JOSEPHUS

THE MAN AND THE HISTORIAN

JOSEPHUS

THE MAN AND THE HISTORIAN

BY

H. ST. JOHN THACKERAY, M.A.

HON. D.D. OXFORD AND DURHAM

WITH A PREFACE BY

GEORGE FOOT MOORE

PROFESSOR OF THE HISTORY OF RELIGION
IN HARVARD UNIVERSITY

INTRODUCTION BY

SAMUEL SANDMEL

KTAV PUBLISHING HOUSE, INC.
NEW YORK

By arrangement with Hebrew Union College—Jewish Institute of Religion.

Originally published as the Hilda Stich Stroock Lectures at the Jewish Institute of Religion. First Published 1929.

Library of Congress Catalogue Card No. 67-18816

Manufactured in United States of America.

DEDICATED TO

GEORGE ALEXANDER KOHUT

SCHOLAR, PATRON OF SCHOLARSHIP,
AND GENEROUS FRIEND

IN GRATEFUL RECOLLECTION OF AN
INTRODUCTION TO AMERICA AND TO
THE JEWISH INSTITUTE OF RELIGION

CONTENTS

INTRODUCTION

The lecture series is quite an old institution in British and American universities. In recent decades it has come to be all the more frequent, despite some inherent difficulties or problems which have occasioned disappointment or even failure. One difficulty is that the scholar is faced by the factors of time, in that the ordinary lecture must be shaped to last approximately an hour, and hence this external consideration, rather than the material itself, can shape a particular lecture. A problem exists in that the audience at a university lecture series can be heterogeneous, and consequently the lecturer has a difficult chore in knowing at just what level to pitch what he has to say.

These potential deficits can be turned into assets, however, as happened in the case of the lectures here reprinted. Mr. Thackeray met the requirement of distilling the essence of his subject, and of putting matters in sharp relief; he met the problem of the nature of the audience by pressing himself towards such a level of clarity that both the student and the mature scholar have gained from his presentation. He met admirably the challenge implicit in a lecture series in that he provided an impressive synthesis of his own matured views in a large and complex field.

Often a lecture series differs in print from the lectures as delivered orally, and not only through that natural rewriting that ensues from the experience of the lecturer in confronting his audience, when the lecturer discerns which sentences or paragraphs can require reformulation or relocation. In common, though not universal practice, the lecturer supplies in the printed version the technical apparatus, footnotes and bibliography, necessarily omitted from the spoken words. Mr. Thackeray's lectures, while they have some scholarly annotation, still retain the form of the spoken word, and appear not to have been greatly recast. The readiest explanation for the sparseness of the scholarly apparatus is that the lectures came at the time when Mr. Thackeray was in the midst of preparing his new translation of *Josephus* for the Loeb Classical series; since that chore obligated him there to provide the full documentation, it is quite understandable that he did not choose to present it in the printed version of this series. One gets the impression, moreover, that these lecutres represent an interim report, and that a fine scholar was taking his audience into his confidence to describe for them some of the considerations which he needed to take account of in working through his project.

In various scholarly fields from time to time there arise great and crucial debates about the interpretation of a body of literature. Such is the case, for example, respecting Philo of Alexandria (20 B.C.-40 A.D.), concerning whose writings antithetical contentions have emerged, both with respect to Philo's significance and with respect to how passages should conceivably be interpreted, and also with respect to the question of how Philo as a totality fits into the context of Judaism in the first Christian century. Respecting Josephus, on the other hand, there have not been any such great upheavals, nor have there been any major novel interpretations. Josephus represents a field of study which from this standpoint might be called unspectacular. While differences of judgment have appeared respecting details here and there, the principal sharp exchanges of opinions have not related to the usual Greek text of Josephus, but rather to passages in the Slavonic Josephus, a controversy about which was relatively new and relatively unsettled at the time that Mr. Thackeray gave his lectures.

The issues relating to Josephus, then, have been relatively minor, and have ordinarily involved extrinsic matters rather than intrinsic ones. For example, it is an extrinsic matter to debate, as scholars have, whether Josephus should be regarded as a loyal Jew or as a traitor to Jews and Judaism. Similarly, it is an extrinsic issue that was raised by Max Krenkel, *Josephus und Lucas,* 1894, as to whether the author of Luke-Acts utilized Josephus as his source of information about early Christianity; this is an intrinsic issue in Luke-Acts rather than in Josephus. Josephus, then, represents a rather stable body of information of consequence and importance, but not an arena for intense scholarly combat.

One omission by Mr. Thackeray is unquestionably deliberate: Mr. Thackeray does not in his lectures provide an explicit statement of the significance and utility of the writings of Josephus, but he assumes that his audience already knows it. Such a concise exposition of the significance of Josephus is to be found, for example, in the article by Samuel Krauss in *The Jewish Encyclopedia,* Vol. VII, pp. 274-281, and especially on page 279. It has seemed to be useful to precede the present reprinting of Thackeray's excellent lectures with a somewhat more detailed statement than that given by Krauss.

For the Christian scholar and the Jewish scholar alike, and for the secular historian as well, whose interest conceivably can focus in the first Christian century, the following might be a statement of the historical significance of that century. At its beginning, Judea, though a Roman possession, was ruled by a king but at its close, kingship disappeared for all time. At its beginning, the Temple in Jerusalem, recently refurbished by Herod, was operative under priests; by the end of the century, the Temple had been destroyed and the priestly families were without significant function. At the beginning of the century, there was that tendency in Judaism which might be called proto-rabbinism, as yet in rather inchoate and beginning stages, with the title rabbi still destined to arise; at the end of the first Christian century, not only had the title of rabbi become frequent, but the role of the rabbi had become dominant, and Rabbinic Judaism was well on its way towards the fullness of its development. In the beginning of the first Christian century, there was as yet no Christianity; at the end of the first Christian century not only had the movement been born but it had come to be separated from its parent, Judaism, and within that century, the figures of Jews and Paul emerged to historical notice, and much of Christian literature had come into existence. The significance of Josephus in regard to the first Christian century in Jewish and Christian scholarship is that he represents the only major source which gives a direct and sequential *historical* account. Manifestly, the New Testament literature and other writings presently to be listed impinge on this history, but the situation can be stated in this way, that the only and full consecutive account of the history of Judea that we have is Josephus'. Were his account to have perished, as did other accounts that we know of, then we would be almost entirely bereft of historical data, and therefore without a knowledge of those events and dates by which other information can be set into some array.

In stressing both the word historical and the phrase, the consecutive writing of history, my intention is to differentiate Josephus from the other bodies of literature which need to be listed. Accordingly, let us hearken back to the phenomenon frequently noted by Bible scholars that whereas the Hebrew Scriptures contain in Samuel and Kings some abundance of information about the pre-exilic period of Jewish history, the Hebrew Scriptures do not provide us with a comparable account of the events of the postexilic period. The consequence is that, by and large, we possess more historical information about the age before 586 than we do about the age that begins around 516. Some of the late books of the Bible, not written in the form of histories, do illumine the late period, but they also provide us with considerable uncertainty and an immense number of enigmas. But there exist other late books, not in the Bible, conventionally referred to as Apocrypha and Pseudepigrapha. This literature seems to come, mostly but not entirely, from the period between the youngest book of the Hebrew Bible, Daniel, written about 150 B.C., and the end of the first Christian century. By Apocrypha there is meant those heterogeneous writings which made their way into the Jewish Greek Bible, but not into the Hebrew; the term Apocrypha in this sense arose in the Protestantism in the 16th century. Roman Catholics regard as canonical those books which Protestants regard as non-canonical, but in our day Catholic scholars too utilize the term Apocrypha, though without subscribing to the Protestant definition of Bible. The Pseudepigrapha are writings of the same general period which did not make their way into either the Hebrew or the Greek Bible. The Pseudepigrapha were assembled only in the 18th century. A listing of the titles of the Apocrypha indicates the character of this literature: III Esdras, IV Esdras, Tobit, Judith, Wisdom of Solomon, Ecclesiasticus, Baruch, the Letter of Jeremiah, the Prayer of Manasseh, I Maccabees, II Maccabees, additions to Esther, and additions to Daniel. A list of the Pseudepigrapha is more difficult to compile since it is a relatively recent collection and not a traditional one; ordinarily it includes the Enoch literature, the Book of Jubilees, the Psalms of Solomon, the Testaments of the Twelve Patriarchs, the Ascension of Isaiah, Apocalypse of Ezra, the Apocalypse of Baruch, the Sybilene Oracles, III and IV Maccabees, and the Lives of the Prophets.

Some of these works, such as I and II Maccabees, are preeminently historical and, as such, not only throw light on the period of the Maccabean revolt which began in 168 B.C., but in turn, are sources which Josephus used. The books which are not written as histories throw light in their own way on the piety of the Jewish religious practices and on the kinds of religious movements that characterized Judaism. Inasmuch as Josephus gives only somewhat more than passing attention to the religious developments and divisions among Jews, the Apocrypha and Pseudepigrapha provide considerably more than the relatively restricted quantity of material that Josephus provides. Much of the content of Apocrypha and Pseudepigrapha goes completely unnoticed in Josephus, and the first immediate impression that a student of Apocrypha and Pseudepigrapha receives is the contrast between the religious accentuation in this material and the concentration on events, especially on royalty and relations with the Romans, which is often Josephus' main concern.

Within Apocrypha and Pseudepigrapha there are writings which give every appearance of being compositions in Greek rather than translations from the Aramaic or Hebrew into Greek. This notice can here lead us to a second body of literature, namely, the Hellenistic Jewish, in which Josephus himself might conceivably be listed. The chief representative of Graeco-Jewish literature is the so-called Septuagint—"so-called," in the sense that modern scholars find it increasingly difficult to isolate one single form which could merit being called *the* Septuagint; in its more conventional usage, however, Septuagint is a term to describe the earliest, or at least an early, translation of the Five Books of Moses into Greek, made approximatly 250 B.C. Later, the rest of the Biblical books were translated. Again, three subsequent translations are known of, because fragments of them have been preserved; they are Aquila, Theodotion, and Symmachus.

Selections from a number of Hellenistic Jewish historians were gathered by Alexander Polyhistor whose dates are 80-40 B.C. Josephus quotes from Alexander's anthology of Graeco-Jewish writers in *Antiquities,* Vol. I, and the fourth-century church historian Eusebius, in *Preparation for the Gospel,* 9:17-39 reproduces a large portion of this assembly of extracts. Names such as Demetrius, Eupolymus, Artapanus, Aristeas, Theoditus and Ezekiel, become more than names which one looks at in the brief fragments that have been perpetuated. Although there is on record a dispute as to whether these items were indeed gathered by Alexander Polyhistor, a frequent view among scholars is that the important thing is that the excerpts *were* gathered and not whether or not Alexander Polyhistor gathered them. We must here notice that there existed other works which have not been preserved, for example a history of the Jewish kings written in the second pre-Christian century by Jason of Cyrene, of which II Maccabees is an epitome, and a first century work by Justus of Tiberius, whose history on the Jewish war against the Romans A.D. 66-70 is totally lost; Josephus in his autobiography polemicizes against this work by Justus. The most eminent name in Graeco-Jewish literature is Philo of Alexandria 20 B.C.-40 A.D., from whose hands have come two works relating to Jewish experiences in Alexandria in the fourth decade of the first century (*Against Flaccus,* and *Legation*) but whose other work is primarily in the realm of religious philosophy. The circumstance that Josephus wrote an apologetic work, called *Against Apion,* necessarily brings into view the writings by some pagans against Judaism and Jews, which writings spurred Josephus to his apology. Indeed the apologetic motif is a factor always to reckon with in all of Josephus' writings, just as it is in the account of the origin of the Jewish translation into Greek which goes under the name of *The Letter of Aristeas* (and also *Pseudo-Aristeas*). So much for Graeco-Jewish literature.

The third body of literature goes under the rubrics of the Rabbinic Writings. In principle these works were to have remained oral and not to have been committed to writing, and for that reason the Jews have perpetuated the paradoxical term for them, namely, the Oral Torah. One might here distinguish among three types of writings. The first is the translation of the Bible into Aramaic called the Targum, usually attributed to one Onkelos. Primarily a literal translation, though with some avoidance of anthropomorphisms and anthropopanthisms, the Targum contains a modicum of interpretation, and from this standpoint is in sharp contrast with a later fragmentary Targum, which is replete with the interpretive expansions. The name ordinarily given to the Aramaic translation of the Prophets, as distinct from the Pentateuch, is the Targum of Jonathan ben Uzziel. The second type of writing, and the principal book, entailing many volumes, is the Talmud. It consists of two distinct parts, reflecting two stages; the first stage is the Mishnah, which reached its written form about 175-200 A.D., and the second stage, the Gemara, which exists in two rescensions, one from Palestine, achieving a written form around 450, and one in Babylon, which was written down around 500. Talmud is basically a legal commentary on the legal portions of Scripture arranged on the basis of topics, such as the Sanhedrin, the New Year, Marriage Contracts, and the like. In its manner, the Talmud, especially the Gemara, hearkens back to sages who flourished at least as early as the first pre-Christian century and, of course, to their successors within the first century.

The third type, the Midrash, differs from the Talmud more in form than content. It follows an arrangement in accordance with the Biblical books, rather than the topical arrangement of the Talmud. The earliest *Midrashim* (the plural of Midrash) are more strictly legal in tone than the later more pietistic and exhortatory Midrashic collections. Since Talmud and Midrash derive from the succession of sages and include allusion to the very earliest of them, pre-Christian and first century rabbis, there are innumerable points of contact with the history narrated in Josephus, despite the circumstance that the rabbinic literature is devoid of any genuine impetus to precise history. Accordingly, there are also a good many items, beginning at least with the age of Alexander Jannaeus, proceeding through the time of Herod, and to the destruction of the Temple in the year 70, wherein one might speak of some overlap between Josephus and rabbinic literature, bearing in mind, however, the important distinction between allusion in legal or pietistic literature and direct historical narration. Quite as significant, however, is a somewhat reversed relationship, namely, that Josephus in his *Antiquities,* in relating the history which is found in the Hebrew Bible, adds many items which reflect his knowledge of the rabbinic tendency to meditate on Scripture and to embellish it with expansions. Thus, for example, Josephus amplifies the biblical material on Abraham with legendary materials found also in the rabbinic writings.

The fourth body of literature would be that of early Christianity, in particular, the Gospels. Matthew allocates the birth of Jesus to the last year of Herod; John the Baptist was executed by Herod Antipas; the Roman procurator is Pontius Pilate; in Luke, Herod Antipas is present in Jerusalem at the trial of Jesus. By and large, the literature of early Christianity abstains from describing the main lines of events in Judea and contents itself with mere allusions. These allusions came to be clear primarily from Josephus, even though at many points (for example, the census described by Luke) difficulties arise in the form of inconsistencies and contradictions when the data in Josephus is consulted.

One must mention a separate category of literature, the sectarian documents from Qumran, usually spoken of as the Dead Sea Scrolls. While much of the controversy over the scrolls and their relationship to Judaism and to early Christianity has receded, notable differences of opinion still exist, and extreme positions still continue to be held by some interpreters. It might be a prudent statement to say that there is at least this almost but not quite universal agreement, that the Scrolls provide additional illumination about religious movements and tendencies in Judaism in the first pre-Christian and the first Christian centuries, to be added to the information which the other bodies of literature disclose.

There is a sense in which the writings of Josephus illumine all these types of writings, and in turn, a sense in which Josephus is himself illuminated or corrected or contended against in aspects of these writings. That scholar whose bent might be to master only one of these bodies of literature nevertheless finds Josephus an inescapably necessary tool. That scholar who may choose to master more than one, or, if it were possible, all these bodies of literature, not only finds Josephus inescapably necessary, but also finds Josephus' writings to be a kind of integrating factor which can bind together the tremendous diversity that these writings represent. It must be emphasized beyond all possible misunderstanding that none of these types of writings gives us a consecutive history such as Josephus provides. Even when we become suspicious about Josephus' reliability and even when we can convict him of contradiction, and of uncontrolled apologetic tendencies, we are faced with the circumstance that if we were to discard or eliminate Josephus, we would virtually be devoid of a clear knowledge of historical events from the beginning of the Maccabean War through the end of the first Christian century.

Because the writings of Josephus represent a historical tool of such tremendous consequence, the lectures by Mr. Thackeray on *Josephus, The Man and the Historian* can serve as an introduction and a set of cautions to that scholar who must inevitably consult Josephus. The translation on which Mr. Thackeray embarked ultimately was published in nine volumes. The first four encompassing *The Life, Against Apion, The Jewish War,* and *The Jewish Antiquities,* Books 1-4, were completed by Mr. Thackeray prior to his death in 1930. For Volume V, Mr. Thackeray had completed translations of *Antiquities,* Book 5 and a portion of Book 6. The remainder of Book 6, and Books 7-8 in Volume V, were completed by the late Ralph Marcus and Allen Wikgren; Marcus carried on the translation through Volume VIII, that is, through Book 16. The last of the volumes, number IX, was published in 1965, and is the work of Louis H. Feldman, who is unquestionably the best authority on Josephus in the United States. The annotations by Mr. Marcus and Mr. Feldman are much richer in their allusion to the first two types of literature, Apocrypha and Pseudepigrapha and Rabbinic Literature, than are the annotations which Mr. Thackeray prepared, for Mr. Thackeray apparently did not know this literature at first hand and was compelled to rely upon chrestomathies and translations. One does not say this in derogation but only in description, for Mr. Thackeray was a classical scholar of wide compass and breadth and of profundity, rather than a scholar in Judaism or Christianity; indeed, his responsibility was more that of translation than of annotation. Moreover, some scholarly tools and books became available subsequent to Mr. Thackeray's embarking on the task, but were not available to him while he was engaged in his work. One can endorse warmly the characterization by the late George Foot Moore in his preface of Mr. Thackeray's great and admirable attainments.

It might not be out of place to comment on two problems which Mr. Thackeray raises. The first of these is the matter of the Slavonic Josephus. In the time that has elapsed, the work of Solomon Zeitlin (*Josephus on Jesus,* Philadelphia, 1931) would seem to have demonstrated the relatively late and unreliable character of the Slavonic version (see Louis H. Feldman's summary in *Studies in Judaica: Scholarship on Philo-Josephus* (1937-1962), Section D, The Slavonic version, pp. 28-30).

Next, on the *Testimonium* itself, which provides the material for Mr. Thackeray's last lecture, "Josephus and Christianity," it is distinctly my impression that Mr. Thackeray's view would today represent only a tiny fraction of current Jewish or Christian opinion. Moreover, if one surveys the handbooks by Christian scholars on early Christianity, one becomes impressed with the relative unimportance of the *Testimonium,* without regard to its possible authenticity or the absence of it. I would suppose that the controversy then raging about the Slavonic Josephus is what prompted the particular lecture, and that it was then timely; it alone of the lectures seems to me to be no longer so. Yet a very recent book, S. G. F. Brandon, *Jesus and the Zealots,* Manchester, 1967, may restore some partial timeliness even to this lecture.

The chief bibliographical tools for the present-day study of Josephus are Ralph Marcus, "Selected Bibliography (1920-1945) of the Jews in the Hellenistic Roman Period," in *Proceedings of the American Academy for Jewish Research,* XVI (1946-47), pp. 97-181 and, most important of all, Louis H. Feldman, *Studies in Judaica: Scholarship on Philo-Josephus* (1937-1962). Feldman provides an annotated bibliography, and his judgments are marked by fairness and responsibility. His essay is by far the most important single essay on Josephus in the past several decades. Special bibliographies are to be found in appendices in various volumes of the Loeb Josephus. Mention should be made of the appearance of the first two volumes of Josephus in a new Greek-German version, annotated, by Otto Michel and Otto Bauernfeind (Bad Hamburg vor der Höhe, 1960 and thereafter).

So far only four parts of the *Lexikon to Josephus,* in which Professor Ralph Marcus collaborated, have been published: Part I, 1930; II, 1934; III, 1948; and IV, 1956. Similarly Ben Zion Wacholder, *Nicolaus of Damascus,* Berkeley, 1962, is a most important tool. Through correspondence with scholars, I learn that the project of bringing up to date, Emil Schuerer, *A History of the Jewish People in the Time of Jesus Christ,* a project in which a number of scholars have joined, is proceeding on its way, but I have not learned about its projected time of completion. Somewhat similarly, an international project, Compendium Rerum Iudaicarum ad Novum Testamentum, has been launched, but is in its very early stages. G. A. Williamson, *The World of Josephus,* Boston, Toronto, 1964, may have some appeal to the general reader, but the serious student will wonder that the same author could have produced the commendable version of *The Jewish War* (Penguin, Baltimore, 1959) and so insignificant a book as his volume on Josephus.

Personal data about Mr. Thackeray has been very elusive. He was born Henry St. John Thackeray in 1869, the son of an Anglican priest, a cousin of William Makepeace Thackeray. He studied at Eton from 1881 to 1887; he won a prize in Mathematics. At Cambridge he studied Classics and Theology; he lectured at Selwyn College from 1894 to 1907. His important works, beyond his translations in the Loeb Classics, are his *St. Paul and the Ancient Jewish Church* (1892); *Grammar of the Old Testament in Greek* (1909); his edition of *The Letter of Aristeas* (1917, revised from an earlier translation which appeared in *Jewish Quarterly Review,* XV (1903), pp. 337-391); *The Septuagint and Jewish Worship,* the Schweich Lectures 1920 (1921); *Some Aspects of the Greek Old Testament,* the Arthur Davis Memorial Lecture (1927). He participated in the *Cambridge Septuagint* (three volumes, 1906-1940) as one of the editors of Volume II.

The Strook Lectures, "Josephus, The Man and the Historian," were given in 1928, and published in 1929. (Three additional series of Hilda Strich Strook Lectures have been published: Hugo Gressmann, THE TOWER OF BABEL, 1927; Charles Cutler Torrey, THE JEWISH FOUNDATIONS OF ISLAM, 1933; Gershom Gerhard Scholem, MAJOR TRENDS IN JEWISH MYSTICISM, 1938.)

Mr. Thackeray passed away on June 30, 1930. A brief obituary appears in the *London Times,* July 4, 1930, page 16.

Samuel Sandmel

PREFACE

IT may well seem to others, as it does to the author of this preface, a work of supererogation to introduce the author of these lectures on Josephus. Those who are acquainted with the volumes which Mr. Thackeray has contributed to the Loeb Classical Library, containing the Autobiography and the book commonly known as "Against Apion," and more recently Books i–iii of the *Jewish War*, not only know him as a skilful translator, but recognize his important contributions to the reconstruction of the Greek text. He has used, as every one must, the great critical edition of Benedict Niese, but with independent judgment. A critical editor, especially of an author as voluminous as Josephus, is naturally inclined, when he has made a *stemma* of the manuscripts, to put in the text the reading which seems to have the best manuscript attestation. Sometimes, instead of making a virtue of necessity, this procedure is represented as the only strictly scientific method, because it eliminates the subjective element in text criticism; but, whatever the sins of earlier editors may have been, who reconstructed a text by guesswork operating on an inadequate apparatus, the methodical elimination of the element of human intelligence can hardly be the ideal of science. The translator, at least, has to consider in individual cases the internal evidence of readings as well as their attestation, and thus in some cases to revise the judgment of the editor. This is what Mr. Thackeray has done in the volumes already published, and in those which are to follow. For this work he has an equipment possessed by none of his predecessors in a concordantial lexicon to the writings of Josephus made for his own use, which, as all scholars will be glad to learn, is presently to be published on the KOHUT FOUNDATION.

The striking differences in the Greek of the various works of Josephus, especially between his earliest work, the *War*, and the Autobiography written near the end of his life, and even within the limits of a single work, as in the *Antiquities*, have long been observed by scholars, and explained in different ways. A more minute investigation of diction and style has led Mr. Thackeray to the conclusion that these differences are chiefly to be attributed to Josephus' literary assistants, or to the default of such assistance. In Books xv–xvi and xvii–xix of the *Antiquities* he has been led to recognize and discriminate two of these assistants, and gives in Lecture V a very interesting account of the method and results of these discoveries.

The sources of Josephus, in the parts of his work which do not fall within his personal knowledge, are the subject of an extensive and constantly growing literature. The question is forced upon us in cases where Josephus traverses the same ground twice, in the *War* and in the *Antiquities*. The criteria which have hitherto been employed have been predominantly historical; the data

are frequently ambiguous, and the opinions of critics
are consequently divergent and even contradictory.   In
Lectures II and III Mr. Thackeray has dealt with some
of these problems with cautious reserve.   He finds an explanation of many of these diversities in the fact that in the
Antiquities Josephus was repeating himself, but wished to
avoid the appearance of copying himself, and accordingly
gave directions to his assistants to vary the expression.
Instances in which the diversity is more substantial
may be accounted for by the changed circumstances of
the author, or by the exigencies of controversy.   That
these considerations furnish a complete explanation,
Mr. Thackeray would of course not maintain; the acquisition of other sources and employment of such in the later
work is an hypothesis for which in some cases strong
probability may be alleged, even though the labors
of Josephus or his editorial assistants have, according to
the literary conventions of the time, given a "Josephan"
form to extracts from other authors.

Some of the problems which have long engaged
critics have in recent years been complicated by the discovery of a so-called "Slavonic" translation of the *War*,
representing a recension sometimes strikingly different
from that of our Greek text. About this Slavonic Josephus
various ingenious hypotheses have been propounded,
such, for example, as that it goes back ultimately to an
"Aramaic" account of the *War* which Josephus says that
he had sent to "the up-country barbarians," probably
meaning what he calls elsewhere the Jews beyond
the Euphrates.   Inasmuch as the Russian Josephus is

demonstrably translated from Greek, it has then further to be supposed that he soon after roughly translated this Aramaic narrative, and that it thus became the basis of what we may perhaps call the first edition of the *War* in Greek, probably under the title Περὶ Ἁλώσεως, The Destruction (of Jerusalem). Toward this and other hypotheses Mr. Thackeray maintains a prudent reserve and an expectant attitude. The question will in fact not be ripe for discussion until a complete critical edition of this version, which is said to be now in preparation, is published, and—for scholars not versed in Old Russian—until a trustworthy translation of the whole is accessible.

An interesting Lecture (IV) is devoted to "Josephus and Judaism," dealing particularly with his Biblical Text. As the author recognizes, the subject is of a kind that does not lend itself well to succinct treatment, and it raises some highly controversial questions, for instance, the use of an Aramaic Targum, and the "Lucianic" (or pre-Lucianic) Greek text in Samuel and the following books, including I Maccabees.

In the last Lecture the much discussed passages in Book xviii of the *Antiquities*, on John the Baptist, James "the brother of the Lord," and on Jesus, are examined with sobriety, and to the argument for the substantial genuineness of the last-named, or at least of a Josephan nucleus, are added some minute observations on the diction and style of the passage. The present phase of the discussion, in which the "Slavonic" Josephus has introduced a new and sensational element, is dealt with in remarks "deliberately brief and non-committal"—

evidently the proper attitude of scholars, in the present state of knowledge, toward far-reaching hypotheses.

Mr. Thackeray's judgment of the character of Josephus, the man, is not flattering, but fairly recognizes the difficulties of a situation into which he had come not wholly by his own fault, but partly, at least, through circumstances beyond his control; his estimate of the historian is more favorable than that of many scholars. It is but just to say that in both aspects Josephus should be assessed by the actualities of his own time and the fashions of contemporary literature, not by the ideals of another age.

The Lectures as a whole are a notable contribution to the subject with which they deal. *The Jewish Institute of Religion* is to be congratulated on such an auspicious inauguration of the Lectures on the HILDA STICH STROOCK FOUNDATION; the gratitude of a wider circle of scholars is due for adding them to its meritorious publications.

Cambridge, Mass.
    April 28, 1928.   GEORGE FOOT MOORE

LIFE AND CHARACTER OF JOSEPHUS: ESTIMATE OF VALUE OF HIS WORKS

I am deeply sensible of the honour which President Wise and the Jewish Institute of Religion have conferred upon me in inviting me to this great country to address you as lecturer on the noble foundation of Mr. Joseph Stroock. I shall recall with pride to the end of my days that I was once the Hilda Stich Stroock Lecturer. I cannot adequately express my sense of the debt which the world of scholarship owes to citizens of America, and more particularly to those who unite to citizenship of the new country the privilege of membership of the ancient people of the Jews. We in England value highly your own original contributions to the advancement of learning: and no less, in difficult times, are we indebted to your generous patrons of literature. A brief personal statement will explain how I come to stand here and serve as a scanty acknowledgement of my obligations to such patronage. Some five years ago I delivered a lecture to the Jews' College in London, in which I referred to a MS Lexicon of Josephus which I had compiled for my own use, with no thought or prospect of publication. That lecture was read by Professor Cadbury, formerly of Harvard University, now of Bryn Mawr, Philadelphia, who urged me to publish the Lexicon and offered to seek financial assistance for the purpose. The result of his kind offices was a generous offer from Dr. George Alexander Kohut to publish the work under the auspices of the Kohut Memorial Fund, and, thanks to him, the Lexicon, which I had contemplated bequeathing in MS to a College Library, will, I hope, ere long see

the light. But Dr. Kohut's liberality did not end there. For in
August last, to my intense surprise and delight, I received through him
an invitation from President Wise to deliver the present course of
lectures. I understand that grounds of health prevented one of your
most illustrious American scholars from addressing you; and my
only regret in standing here is that I cannot hope to provide such
entertainment as you would have received from Dr. George Foot
Moore, whose latest great work on " Judaism " has charmed and
instructed all readers. I need only add that I have been a life-long
lover and student of Jewish antiquities, and in particular of two
collections of documents which were the principal channels for
diffusing a knowledge of Judaism to the ancient world—the Greek
Bible, known as the Septuagint, and the works of Josephus.

I am conscious of my temerity in attempting to address you on
your own national historian. But indeed Josephus has always found
more friends among Christians than among his own countrymen;
and amid the animosities to which his career has given rise, hated
by Jews as a renegade and turncoat, belauded by Christians on the
strength of a debatable passage on their Master in the *Antiquities*, it
is possible that an outsider, albeit a Christian, may be in a position to
form a more impartial estimate of his life-work than a compatriot.
For, as will appear later, I am not biassed in his favour by my
interpretation of that particular passage. The importance of his
works is undeniable and it is to Christians that we owe their
preservation. The controversial question of his attitude to Christianity has perhaps obscured and belittled his sterling merits as a
patriot and apologist for Judaism. I am not blind to his faults.
As his translator for the Loeb Classical Library—that priceless boon
to scholarship from another of your public-spirited American bene-
factors, Dr. James Loeb—it has been my lot to have Josephus as a
daily companion for some years; and his company, I confess, has
not been a wholly unmixed pleasure. His faults are obvious, but
there are many compensations. However, I will reserve my estimate
of his character and writings until later.

The study of Josephus has latterly entered on a new phase. There was a time in my own country when almost every house possessed two books, a Bible and a Josephus, in the old eighteenth century version of William Whiston. That period of general and undiscriminating popularity has passed, but has been succeeded by an age of more scientific inquiry. The beginning of this new age is marked by the appearance of the great critical edition of Benedict Niese, now nearly 40 years ago. The twentieth century has seen the publication in instalments of an invaluable French annotated translation, now nearing completion, from M. Theodor Reinach and his collaborators. From Germany, again, we have had a highly suggestive and revolutionary study of the historian from Herr Richard Laqueur,[1] and an interesting investigation of the sources of the *Jewish War* from Wilhelm Weber.[2] The battle over the authenticity of the *testimonium* has been reopened, with Eduard Norden as protagonist on the attacking side, and Harnack and Burkitt as doughty champions for the defence. Lastly, from the unfortunate land of Russia comes new evidence which may prove revolutionary and is anyhow likely to provide controversy for years to come—the disclosure of a Slavonic version of the *Jewish War*, containing further strange allusions to John the Baptist, Jesus and the early Christians, and regarded by some leading authorities as derived from the original, unexpurgated, draft of the Jewish historian. That problem is still *sub judice*, but it has already awakened a revived interest in our author.

My subject is Josephus, the man and the historian, rather than the age in which he lived; but some allusion to the background of the previous and contemporary history is unavoidable. It was a momentous age for his nation and for the world. There was, as we learn from pagan historians, a widespread and deep-seated belief throughout the whole of the East that a person or persons issuing

---

[1] *Der jüdische Historiker Fl. Josephus*, Gießen, 1920.
[2] *Josephus und Vespasian*, Berlin, 1921.

from Judaea were destined at that time to rule the world. That belief was doubtless a main factor in fostering the passionate desire of a large section of the nation for independence and promoting the struggle with Rome which ended in catastrophe. The preliminary events that led up to that struggle will be familiar to you and I need merely mention a few outstanding landmarks. The glorious period of the Hasmonaean house, when for a time, under the successors of Judas Maccabaeus, Israel regained some faint reflection of the splendour of the age of David, ended too soon in the quarrels of the brothers Aristobulus and Hyrcanus, and the appeal to Rome as mediator. The die was cast. Aristobulus proving recalcitrant, Pompey in 63 B.C. took Jerusalem, and Syria became a Roman province, Hyrcanus retaining a nominal sovereignty as vassal of Rome. But the last of the Hasmonaeans was overshadowed and gradually ousted from his throne by the rise of the Idumaean usurpers, Antipater and his son Herod. Then followed the long reign of Herod the Great, a period of external magnificence under Roman patronage, internally an age of oppression and growing resentment of the nation against their rulers. On Herod's death in 4 B.C. the smouldering fires broke into flame. In Rome Archelaus, the nominated heir, had to fight for confirmation of his title before Augustus against deputations of his countrymen clamouring for independence, while in Palestine he had to contend with various rival claimants to the throne. After 10 years of misrule Archelaus was deposed in 6 A.D. and Judaea was annexed to the province of Syria and placed under Roman procurators. From this time dates the rise of the Zealots, the anti-Roman extremists, "the fourth sect" as Josephus calls them, and responsible, in his judgment, for all the horrors of the final catastrophe. It was the coming of Quirinius in 6–7 A.D. to take a valuation of the property of the newly annexed district, which led to the revolt of Judas of Galilee and his companions. "They asserted," writes Josephus,[3] "that the valuation meant nothing less than downright slavery, and exhorted the nation

[3] *Ant.* xviii. 4.

to rally in defence of their liberty." It was the exhortation of this band of fanatical patriots, assisted by the excesses and extortionate rapacity of the last of the Roman procurators, which 60 years later led to the outbreak of open war.

For the life of Josephus we are wholly dependent on the historian's own statements, contained partly in an incomplete autobiography published towards the end of his life, partly in scattered notices in his *Jewish War*. The autobiography is a disproportionate work, the major part of it being devoted to the period of some six months during which the author held command, or some sort of commission, in Galilee prior to the coming of Vespasian's army; to this, brief sketches of the earlier and later personal history are appended as prologue and epilogue. The reason for this disproportion is that the work is an *apologia*, put out in reply to the damaging criticisms of a rival historian, Justus of Tiberias, who, in his history, which appeared towards the end of the first century, attempted to throw the responsibility for the war, or at least for the revolt of his native city, Tiberias, upon Josephus. The history of Justus has not survived, and we have unfortunately no check upon the statements of our author other than his own, which are far from consistent. For we have a second overlapping account of this period in the *Jewish War*. Here there are unaccountable discrepancies, and the autobiographical notices of the historian in connexion with the outbreak of hostilities must be pronounced the least trustworthy portion of his writings. The numerous inconsistencies, of a minor or a graver character, between the two accounts of his command in Galilee, betray either gross carelessness or actual fraud, and it is to be feared that he cannot be wholly exonerated from the latter charge. His critics forced him to admit some facts which he had not merely, as he himself says,[4] "suppressed," but, it appears, actually distorted. Where the two accounts disagree, that in the autobiography probably comes nearer to the truth; of the genesis of that work I shall have more to say later. With the exception of that critical half-year in

[4] *Vita* 338.

Galilee, we have no reason to doubt the general accuracy of the author's sketch of his career.

Of a priestly family and with royal blood in his veins on the mother's side, Joseph ben Matthias was born in the year of the accession of Gaius (Caligula), 37–38 A.D., just half way through that stormy era which intervened between the rise of the Zealots under Judas of Galilee in the year 6 and the outbreak of the war with Rome in 66. We do not know the precise year of his death, but it probably fell in the early years of the second century, and we may say that his life was divided by the Great War into two approximately equal portions: thirty-three years of stress spent in Palestine as priest, general and prisoner, and a period of comparative calm passed by the Roman citizen and man of letters, Flavius Josephus, in the capital of the Empire.

In the year before his birth the Roman procurator Pontius Pilate had been recalled from Judaea: Herod Agrippa I had just received his liberty and a portion of his grandfather's kingdom from the new emperor. The lad's memory would recall the scenes of excitement aroused in Palestine by the mad attempt of Caligula to erect his statue in the Temple, when the outbreak of war was narrowly averted by the procrastination of the Roman governor, Petronius, to execute the order, and the timely death of the emperor. Of his education, the historian tells us that his precocious talents, at the age of 14, brought learned Rabbis to consult him, and how, two years later, he entered on what might be called his short university course, when he studied the tenets of the three national sects, Pharisees, Sadducees and Essenes. The unworldly, monastic life of the last-named community, of whom he has left us a full and appreciative account in the *War*, had a special attraction for him at this time and left an indelible impression. This cosmopolitan man of affairs seems to have had a genuine strain of asceticism in his nature. At any rate he followed up his course in Jerusalem by three years of monastic life in the desert. " Not content," he writes,[5] "with the

[5] *Vita* 11.

Some six months elapsed between the disaster of Cestius in the autumn of 66 and the arrival of Vespasian's avenging army in Palestine in the spring of 67. Josephus now reappears upon the scene and his proceedings during this half-year in Galilee, which was to bear the first brunt of the war, practically fill the narrative. But though he has left us two accounts of this period, one in the *Autobiography* exceptionally full, the other a briefer sketch in his *Jewish War*, the discrepancies between them make it exceedingly difficult to reconstruct the history and to discover his real aims and policy. His conduct at the time was severely censured by a rival leader, John of Gischala, who tried to get him superseded: it was censured again some thirty years later by a rival historian, Justus of Tiberias, whose damaging criticisms in his lost History of the War called forth our author's Autobiography. A lack of candour, the equivocal position of a pacifist driven to take up arms, and an endeavour at one time to ingratiate himself with the Roman conquerors and their *protégé*, King Agrippa II, at another to reply to his Jewish critics, have combined to produce a confused narrative. The double account was the starting-point for a fresh and stimulating, if somewhat fanciful, study of the historian's life produced some years ago by Herr Richard Laqueur. In one point at least I think Laqueur is right, namely that in the *Life* we come nearer to the actual facts. The questions arising are two: what were the motives of Josephus? What was his commission and did he exceed it? There is an initial discrepancy on the subject of his commission. In the *War* we read [14] that the Jews, on their return from the rout of Cestius, assembled in the temple and appointed additional generals to conduct the campaign. "Joseph son of Gorion and Ananus the high priest were elected to the supreme control 'of the affairs' with a special charge to raise the height of the walls." The country was divided between six territorial generals, Josephus being named last: "Josephus son of Matthias was given the two Galilees with the addition of Gamala, the strongest city in that region."

ii. 562–568.

experience thus gained, on hearing of one named Bannus, who dwelt in the wilderness, wearing only such clothing as trees provided (i. e. bark), feeding on such things as grew of themselves, and using frequent ablutions of cold water, by day and night, for purity's sake, I became his devoted disciple." From this Hemerobaptist, as we may call him, he may possibly have learned something of the tenets of a kindred spirit, the forerunner of Christianity, John the Baptist. But Josephus was not destined to remain an anachorite, and on his return to Jerusalem at the age of 19 he definitely attached himself to the Pharisees.

Of his early manhood he relates one outstanding event, his visit at the age of 26 or 27, in the year 64, to Rome, the city that was for so long to be his home. The ostensible object of this visit was a charitable one—the liberation of certain priests of his acquaintance, who on some trifling charge had been sent up by Felix, the procurator of Judaea, to be tried by Nero. On this errand he was successful, through the influence of the disreputable agents whose aid was necessary, the favourite Jewish actor Aliturus, and the infamous Poppaea, once mistress, now wife of the Emperor and all-powerful at court. This notorious woman had coquetted with Judaism, and in virtue of these leanings to his race is elsewhere dignified by our historian with the epithet of "god-fearing" (θεοσεβής).[6] It is idle to attempt, as others have done, to link this visit on to contemporary events and Christian history in particular. One writer [7] wished to connect the liberation of the Jewish priests with the liberation of the Apostle Paul who a few years earlier had been sent up by Festus for trial and, like Josephus, had suffered shipwreck *en route*. The year 64 was the year of the burning of Rome and of the persecution of the Christians, who were accused of incendiarism; and another writer [8] has darkly hinted that the gifts which were showered by Poppaea on Josephus were a bribe to secure his aid in the cause.

[6] *Ant.* xx. 195.
[7] Edersheim, art. "Josephus" in Dict. of Christian Biography.
[8] Corrsen, *Zeitschrift für die N. T. Wissenschaft*, 1914, p. 139 f.

Both suggestions are baseless; but we may legitimately speculate whether the visit to the capital had not some ulterior motive in connexion with the war impending over his own country.

At any rate it had impressed him with a sense of the invincible might of Rome, and on his return to Judaea, where he found his countrymen smarting under the last of the procurators and heading for revolt, he vainly endeavoured to pacify the war party. Finding himself powerless to restrain them and fearing as he says, that his reiterated warnings would bring him into odium and the suspicion of siding with the enemy, he was forced to seek asylum for a time in the Temple; on issuing from which he and his friends, unable to check the rebels "professed to concur in their views," seeking merely to persuade them to act on the defensive and leave the Romans to make the first move. "In doing so," he writes, "we had hopes that ere long Cestius (the governor of Syria) would come up with a large army and quell the revolution." [9]

I must pass lightly over the scenes leading up to the outbreak of hostilities, of which Josephus has left us a vivid picture, but in which he himself played no leading part. It was the tyranny and rapacity of the Roman procurator which set the flames alight. A very different character from the Petronius who had averted war under Caligula, Florus was only anxious to fan the flames in order to cover up his own enormities under the larger calamity. There were two storm-centres, Caesarea, the seat of the Roman governor, and Jerusalem; and at both places Florus did his best to provoke trouble. The quarrels at Caesarea between the Jewish and Syrian inhabitants were part of a larger movement, a wave of anti-Jewish feeling which at this time swept over all the cities of Syria, as well as Egyptian Alexandria. At Caesarea a long standing dispute, in which the Jews claimed that the city was theirs in virtue of its founder, Herod the Great, had just ended in an appeal to Nero and a decree in favour of the Graeco-Syrian population. Here the ostensible pretext for war was a trivial incident—the wilful blocking of the

[9] *Vita* 20 ff.

approach to a Jewish Synagogue by a Greek builder. The Jewish notables appealed to Florus and offered him eight talents to procure the cessation of the work. Florus accepted the money, promised assistance, and forthwith quitted the place, "leaving" as Josephus says, [10] "a free field to sedition, as though he had sold the Jews a licence to fight the matter out." At Jerusalem, his conduct was similar, and a raid on the temple treasury was the last straw. A storm of indignation arose; and with grim humour some wa in the crowd carried round a basket begging coppers for the gov nor, as for an unfortunate pauper. [11] I need not dwell on sequel: the retaliatory measures of Florus for the insults offe him, the appeals to Cestius, the vain efforts of the priestly ar classes to stave off revolution, the great speech to the citizens which is put into the mouth of King Agrippa, to submit to Florus and the expulsion of Agrippa, the s castle of Antonia by the rebels, the siege laid to the R in Herod's Palace, their capitulation and perfidious m contemporaneous massacre "on the same day and as by the hand of providence," writes Josephu inhabitants of Caesarea by their fellow-citizens

The second scene in the drama opens with Gallus, the governor of Syria, upon Jerus northern suburb of Bezetha, and then on th at a moment when "had he decided," w his way through the walls, he would h with and the war would have been ov table retreat, the pursuit of the J Romans in the passes of Bethhoron the conversion of the retreat int wholly recovered from that disg victory of the weaker nation h were assembled. It recalls in

[10] *B.J.* ii. 288.   [11] *ib.* 29
[12] *ib.* 457.   [13] *ib.* 5

To set beside this, we have the following statement in the *Life*: [15] "After the defeat of Cestius, the leading men in Jerusalem, observing that the brigands [16] and revolutionaries were well provided with arms, feared that, being without weapons themselves, they might be left at the mercy of their adversaries, as in fact eventually happened. Being informed, moreover, that the whole of Galilee had not yet revolted from Rome, and that a portion of it was still tranquil, they dispatched me with two other priests, Joazar and Judas, men of excellent character, to induce the disaffected to lay down their arms and to impress upon them the desirability of reserving these for the picked men of the nation. The latter, so it was decided, were to have their weapons constantly in readiness for future contingencies, but should wait and see what action the Romans would take."

Thus, in the *War* Josephus is represented as military commander of Galilee from the outset: in the *Life* the young priest of 29 is sent, with two other priests, probably his seniors, on a pacific mission to disarm the hotheads and endeavour to keep the peace. No mention is made until later of his holding supreme command, and he may originally have been in a subordinate position. Did he act *ultra vires*? Possibly: at any rate he was represented as doing so. The picture drawn in the *War* of his appointment at the outset to an important military post was more suited to Roman ears, as was also the account which he there gives of his training an army on Roman lines: [17] "he understood that the Romans owed their invincible strength above all to discipline and military training; if he despaired of providing similar instruction, to be acquired only by long use, he observed that their discipline was due to the number of their officers, and he therefore divided his army on Roman lines and increased the number of his company commanders," and so on.

Where he acquired his knowledge of Roman methods and tactics does not appear: it is a different picture which is drawn in the *Life*. There we are told that he failed in the object of his mission, the

<hr/>

[15] *Vita* 28 f.   [16] The constant term for the anti-Roman extremists.
[17] *B.J.* ii, 577 ff.

disarmament of the rebels: " I summoned the most stalwart of the brigands and, seeing that it would be impossible to disarm them, persuaded the people to pay them as mercenaries," binding them by oath " not to enter the district unless they were sent for or their pay was in arrear, and dismissing them with injunctions to refrain from attacking either the Romans or their neighbours." [18] He further dismisses his priestly colleagues, who are represented as intent only on collecting their tithes, possibly for war-funds, and not merely, as Josephus states, to fill their own pockets. Then ensues a long struggle with a commanding figure, destined to play a large part in the siege of Jerusalem, and now a rival for leadership in Galilee and depicted as an arch-villain, John of Gischala. John represents to his friends at Jerusalem that Josephus is aiming at a τυραννίς, and entreats them to induce the assembly to deprive him of his command and appoint him (John) in his stead. The high priest Ananus and Simon, son of Gamaliel, of whom Josephus speaks in high terms and obviously stood in awe, are induced to send a secret deputation of four, including apparently one of our historian's former colleagues (Joazar), to supersede him. Josephus outwits this deputation, makes counter-representations to Jerusalem and gets himself reinstated, or, perhaps we should say, his position regularized.

If we attempt to fathom the policy and motives of Josephus at this period, we can only say that he was playing a double, waiting game, possibly still vainly hoping to avert war by some form of compromise. The selection of the young priest, with known pacifist and pro-Roman tendencies, to this important post is mysterious. He had a distracted province. Sepphoris, the capital, remained staunchly pro-Roman (though even this statement is once contradicted), but significantly refused to have any dealings with Josephus: Gamala was also induced to remain loyal: Tiberias was a scene of faction and a source of constant trouble and personal risk to Josephus. Of preparations for war we hear of his training of

[18] *Vita* 77 f.

volunteers, and of fortification of cities and villages under his personal superintendence; lists of these places, not quite identical, are proudly paraded by our author in his two narratives. On the other hand, some of his statements leave us in doubt on which side his sympathies lay, as when, in reply to a request from John of Gischala to authorize him to seize the imperial corn stored in the villages of Upper Galilee, he tells us, in support of his refusal, "I intended to reserve the corn *either for the Romans* or for my own use." [19] No wonder such a general was suspected of harbouring designs of betraying the country to the enemy. But it was the rebels and extremists, whom he had been sent to disarm, the "brigands" (λῄσται) as they are constantly called, who dominated the situation. They forced his hands and compelled him, if he was not to be superseded, to put himself at the head of the war party.

Here the author's *Jewish War* takes up the story. On the advance of Vespasian from Antioch in the spring of 67, Josephus, deserted by most of his army of volunteers, threw himself into the fortified town of Jotapata, "deliberately entering a prison" as the Roman general remarked,[20] and decided to stand a siege. Of the 47 days' siege—his brief period of military fame—the fall of the town (July 67), his capture by the Romans after a narrow escape from being murdered by his companions in hiding, and his prophecy of Vespasian's rise to imperial power, he has left us a graphic account. Perhaps I may be allowed to recall to you the familiar scene in the cave in some of his own words. The hiding-place has been discovered, and Josephus is just about to surrender to the Roman officer sent to fetch him, when he is prevented by his compatriots who threaten to kill him. Thereupon he harangues them in a long rhetorical speech on the iniquity of suicide, which it is incredible that they would have tolerated. "But," says Josephus,[21] "desperation stopped their ears, for they had long since devoted themselves to death" and they ran at him from this side and that, sword in hand. "But he, addressing one by name, fixing

[19] *Vita* 72.   [20] *B.J.* iii. 144.   [21] *B.J.* iii. 384 ff.

his general's eye of command upon another, clasping the hand of a third, shaming a fourth by entreaty, and, torn by all manner of emotions at this critical moment, succeeded in warding off from his throat the blades of all, turning like a wild beast surrounded by the hunters to face his successive assailants. Even in his extremity, they still held their general in reverence; their hands were powerless, their swords glanced aside, and many, in the act of thrusting at him, spontaneously dropped their weapons. But, in his straits, his resource did not forsake him. Trusting to God's protection, he put his life to the hazard ": he proposes the drawing of lots to decide the order of mutual destruction. " The proposal inspired confidence; his advice was taken and he drew lots with the rest. Each man thus selected presented his throat to his neighbour, in the assurance that his general was forthwith to share his fate; for sweeter to them than life was the thought of death with Josephus. He, however (should one say by fortune or by the providence of God?) was left alone with one other; and, anxious neither to be condemned by the lot nor, should he be left to the last, to stain his hand with his countryman's blood, he persuaded this man also, under a pledge, to remain alive."

By what jugglery of the lots he escaped on this occasion we cannot precisely say. But if the Slavonic text may be trusted as preserving his original account of this ignoble episode, he did in his first edition unblushingly admit that there was jugglery. Instead of the pious remark, " Should one say by fortune or by the providence of God?," we are there told that "he counted the numbers with cunning and thereby misled them all." The prisoner is then brought up to Vespasian, and his veracity in what follows is above suspicion. His prediction that Vespasian would shortly become emperor is attested by a pagan witness [22] and is moreover too closely embedded in the narrative, being the occasion of the prisoner's subsequent release, to be a fiction. He must at least be credited with a sagacious reading of the signs of the times. The prediction has indeed been

[22] Suetonius, *Vesp.* 5.

attributed to a man of a very different type, Johanan ben Zakkai,[23] and the Rabbis in this instance have not scrupled to transfer the prophet's honours to a more popular hero.

Henceforth in Roman hands, first as prisoner, then as onlooker, reporter, interpreter and mediator, Josephus was now in comparative security. Hostilities were partially suspended during the eventful year 68–69, the year of the four emperors, which saw the death of Nero and, in rapid succession, the promotion of three successors. In July 69 Vespasian's legions took matters into their own hands and proclaimed him emperor. One of the first acts of his reign was the liberation of his Jewish prisoner, whose prediction had now come true. Accompanying Vespasian to Alexandria, Josephus possibly availed himself of the opportunity of his brief stay in that city to accumulate some of that Alexandrian lore of which he shows a knowledge in his writings. Thence he returned with Titus to the siege of Jerusalem and witnessed the end. His services as mediator, to go the round of the walls and counsel submission, were constantly requisitioned by Titus, and he was not yet out of peril, bitterly hated by the Jewish Zealots, and suspected of treachery by the Romans whenever they met with a reverse. After the *débâcle* he was presented by Titus with a tract of land outside Jerusalem and some "sacred books"; he also obtained the liberation of a number of his friends. He then accompanied the conqueror to Rome.

Of his thirty or more years spent in Rome there is little to record. The client of the Flavians and commissioned to write the history of their triumph, he was awarded the rights of Roman citizenship, a lodging in the former palace (*privata aedes*) of Vespasian and one of the pensions newly instituted by that emperor.[24] He witnessed the triumphal procession of the conquerors, with what feelings we are left to imagine, and must have

[23] Abot de-R. Nathan 4, 5, quoted by Moore, *Judaism* ii. 116.
[24] *Vita* 423: Suet., *Vesp.* 18.

seen the new Rome arising from the ashes in which the fire of
Nero and the civil war had left it. The sedentary life of the
historian, uneventful after the stirring scenes of the past, was only
diversified by the attacks to which he was constantly exposed from
his countrymen, including his own household. He was accused of
subsidizing a Jewish revolt in Cyrene, he was slandered by his
son's tutor, and in his closing years came the attack of his rival
Justus, whose damaging exposures threatened both his position of
security and the sale of his works. The death of Titus in 79 marks
a change for the worse in his external surroundings and a new
departure in his literary activity. Deprived of his honoured patron,
he shakes off the Roman fetters and becomes the historian and
apologist of his nation. But the hated deserter could never regain
the affection of his countrymen: it was Rome that perpetuated
his memory. We learn from Eusebius [25] that his statue was erected
in the city and his works placed in the public library.

His domestic life, as is not surprising in an egoist of his character,
had its matrimonial troubles. He was married at least three times,
being deserted by one wife and divorcing another.[26]

To this brief sketch of our author's career I have only two
subjects on which I would touch to-day. The first is a literary
problem, relating to the origin of the Autobiography; the second
is the more difficult task of attempting to estimate the historian's
character.

The Autobiography comes to us as one of the latest of his
writings, produced when the author was well over 60. It alludes
to the death of Agrippa II which we know from another source [27]
took place in the year 100. "Why," he says, addressing Justus
who had brought out a belated history of the war, "why did you
not publish it in the lifetime of the emperors Vespasian and Titus ...
and while King Agrippa and all his family ... were still among
us?" [28] The *Life*, which is in reality an *apologia pro vita sua*, was

---

[25] *Hist. eccles.* iii. 9.   [26] *Vita* 415, 426 f.   [27] Photius.   [28] *Vita* 359.

called into existence by the appearance of this rival history, in defence of the author's conduct in Galilee more than thirty years before. It was not issued as an independent work, but attached as an appendix to the author's *magnum opus,* the *Antiquities,* or rather to a second or later edition of that work. That a modern book has reached a second edition may be indicated by the existence of two prefaces. In the work of Josephus a similar inference may be drawn from the peroration. The *Antiquities* has two perorations. In that which stands first he writes[29] "But here my *Archaeology* shall cease," and then, after telling us what a fine achievement it is, he continues: "But perhaps it will not be taken amiss if I give a brief sketch of my family and the events of my life, while there are still persons alive either to convict or to corroborate me." The *Vita,* as I said, is later than 100 A.D. and this peroration must also have been penned in the second century. But then a new summing up begins. A second time he writes "But here I will close my *Archaeology,*" and names the number of lines (στίχοι) in the work, some future literary projects, and the date of writing, "the thirteenth year of the reign of Domitian," i.e. 93–4 A.D. Here we have the older peroration to the first edition, dating from the last decade of the first century, but now relegated to the end.

But, though we know that the *Life* was not issued until the 2nd century, a theory has recently been propounded by Herr Laqueur, which would make the kernel of the *Vita* not the latest, but the very earliest work of our author, written at the age, not of 65, but of 30. In Laqueur's opinion the nucleus of the *Vita* is an official report of the writer's conduct of affairs in Galilee drafted, before the siege of Jotapata, for submission to the Jerusalem authorities. It is his defence against the charge brought against him by John of Gischala of acting *ultra vires* and aiming at a despotism. This unliterary report, unpublished at the time, was in after years produced from the author's papers and utilized to meet the attack of Justus: details were modified, a prologue and epilogue appended

---

[29] *Ant.* xx. 259.

Thackeray.

2

and the whole was worked up into an autobiography. The theory is based partly on the disproportionate space devoted to the Galilaean period, partly on the incongruity and inconsistencies in the narrative, and in particular on a comparison of those passages in the *Life* and in the *War* where the two accounts overlap. In these cases three *strata* of different dates may, according to this view, be distinguished. There is first the youthful report, approaching nearest to the truth. The historian is sent on a pacific mission to Galilee, not as commander-in-chief; John of Gischala is still a friend, not an enemy; the great war that is impending is not named as such, nor even envisaged; the reader is not referred to the parallel narrative in the *Bellum Judaicum* which was not yet written. Secondly, we have the story as adapted in the *Jewish War* for his patrons, the Romans and King Agrippa: the author is represented as commander-in-chief from the outset, and so on. Lastly, we have the narrative re-edited and modified to meet the attack of Justus—the *Vita* as finally issued.

It is an attractive theory. That Josephus kept some contemporary record of his period of office for his own use, or was required to submit a formal report to the authorities in Jerusalem, is not at all improbable. The theory would account for some of the incongruities in different portions of the *Vita*. It might also, I was once inclined to think, account for the crudity of the style, which is strangely in contrast with the polished Greek of the other production of our author's old age—the *contra Apionem*. If Laqueur were right, we should have an interesting relic of the historian's youthful style before he had the benefit of literary assistance in Rome. Laqueur's stimulating essay has thrown much new light on our author's career, the stages in his development, and his methods of work. In particular, he has, I think, established the fact that he was constantly revising his earlier writings. But the German critic has not submitted his theory to the searching test of phraseology, which fails to bear out his distinction between "early" and "late" portions in the *Vita*. In compiling a Lexicon to Josephus I have minutely investigated the author's language, and the theory, as stated, seems to break down owing to the numerous links of style, which connect the *Life as a whole* with the last book of the *Antiquities*, suggesting contemporaneous composition. The style of Josephus' writings is uneven; there are well-marked *strata*, due to the employment of various assistants, now of one, now of another, while occasionally the author seems to be thrown back on his own unaided resources. As will be shown in a later lecture, Books xv and xvi of the *Antiquities* are the work of one assistant, xvii–xix of another; but in Book xx and in the *Vita* we appear to have the *ipsissima verba* of the historian. At any rate, these two books are closely united not only by the express announcement at the close of the *Antiquities* of the author's intention to append a *curriculum vitae,* but by the internal evidence of style. Only in these two books do we find phrases like "no small alarm," "quell disturbances," "when I saw to what a plight (μέγεθος) of misery they were come" and many more; these parallels extend over the whole of the *Life,* including Laqueur's alleged "early" portions. His thesis is therefore only tenable on the supposition that the youthful "report" to the Jerusalem authorities, like the first draft of the *War,* was written in Aramaic and afterwards in later life reproduced in Greek. If presented in that form, which Laqueur himself rejects, the theory seems to me unobjectionable and not improbable.

It remains for me to attempt some estimate of the man and his work. It will be evident that his is not a wholly amiable, still less an heroic, character, and that as a writer he lacks some of the essential qualifications of the great historian. Egoist, self-interested, time-server and flatterer of his Roman patrons, he may be justly called: such defects are obvious. He was not one to sacrifice his life in a great cause: no warlike liberator of his country like Judas Maccabaeus, no Ezra or Johanan ben Zakkai to recreate a new Judaism on the ruins of the past, no Thucydides to record the tragedy of his nation with strict and sober impartiality. Yet

2*

for all this we must not be led to exaggerate his failings or to underestimate his sterling merits and his immense contribution to learning and our knowledge of the past.

His worst enemies, in his lifetime and since, have, I think, always been found among his own countrymen; and the rancour displayed against the "turncoat" or "Romanist" (*Römling*), as he is often called, is intelligible. I do not know whether his latest biographer, Herr Laqueur, is a Jew, but the black portrait which he has drawn inclines me to think so. I owe much to the work of this brilliant critic, but I think he has carried the process of denigration too far. His imaginative reconstruction of the history is based on a distinction between "early" and "late" portions in our author's works, which is far from certain and not sustained by any marked change in style. In particular, the sketch of our author's career in Galilee—those six months which bulk so largely in his life, against which we are always brought up and which seem to hang like a mill-stone about his neck—is highly fanciful. According to Laqueur, the success of the youthful Josephus on a diplomatic mission to Rome obtained for him almost immediately another important mission in Galilee. It was a pacific mission, to disarm the Zealots: war with Rome was as yet hardly on the horizon, and no generals had yet been appointed. Finding the "brigands" too strong for him, he paid them to keep quiet. His colleagues, having failed to execute their commission, loyally returned to Jerusalem: Josephus remained, now a rebel against authority, and set himself up as a despot. But his hands were forced by the insurgents, who drove him into war with Rome. He put himself at the head of the rebels and then, by his self-surrender at Jotapata, betrayed them. But, as the original organizer of the revolt, he was largely responsible for the ultimate fall of Jerusalem. His narrative in the *Jewish War* is a distorted version of the events, written under Roman direction and patronage.

Much of this reconstruction of the Galilaean episode seems to me highly questionable. To begin with, there is no apparent connexion between the missions to Rome and to Galilee. Herr Laqueur ignores the period of upwards of two years which intervened, crowded with incidents, including the massacre of the Roman garrison in Jerusalem, the march of Cestius upon the city, his retreat and the rout of his legion in the defiles of Bethhoron. Those events made the Great War inevitable: Rome could not possibly leave such insults unavenged, and the victors of Cestius must have made some immediate preparations against impending hostilities, including presumably the appointment of generals. Whether Josephus was given military command at that period is uncertain, and much of his career in Galilee remains obscure. But the charges of rebellion against his superiors in Jerusalem and of aiming at a despotism seem to me highly disputable. He seems to have consulted and kept in touch with the Jerusalem authorities throughout, and the secret attempts to supersede him were promptly followed by his formal reinstatement. I should doubt whether he had any ambition for political leadership.

Looking at his career as a whole, I do not think that a lack of patriotism can be reckoned among his faults. His lamentations in his works over his country's fate, his oral exhortations beneath the walls of the besieged capital and the exhortations which he puts into the mouth of others, were sincere. He was [30] a pacifist, without the strength of character to control the militants, who had no use for a mediator. Who indeed could have controlled those hot-heads? And who can say how the course of history might have been changed had his counsels prevailed? As a *religio licita* Judaism had little to gain and everything to lose by revolution. Nor can I forget that Josephus does not stand alone in seeing an overruling destiny in the ordering of events: the doom of the city had been pronounced by Another before him. The Jewish historian was involved in early manhood in the rush of momentous events

[30] I repeat here in part what I said in a previous lecture delivered in 1923 at *Jews' College*, London, and printed in *Judaism and the Beginnings of Christianity* (Routledge).

and overwhelmed by a wave of national feeling which had long been gathering force, which he could not stem and vainly strove to direct. Recognising from the first the hopelessness of defying imperial Rome and striving to avert catastrophe by compromise, he nevertheless, under pressure of circumstances, threw himself into the task of organising, to the best of his ability, the defences of Galilee, while resistance was possible. At the siege of Jerusalem he was unremitting in his efforts to stave off the final catastrophe by counselling surrender; and then, after the *débâcle,* when as the client of the conquerors he might have been tempted to disown his nation, he devoted the energies of his later life to writing an elaborate history of it and championing its cause against the slanders of a malignant world. His fine *apologia* for Judaism, the *contra Apionem,* crowns his services to his race. He has surely earned the name of patriot.

An estimate of his merits and defects as a writer must be reserved for my next two lectures on the *Jewish War* and the *Jewish Antiquities.* In the sequel I propose to consider the extent of the influence exercised upon him by his various surroundings, in other words to attempt to estimate his relationship to his native Judaism, his adopted Hellenism, and to Christianity.

THE "JEWISH WAR"

Yesterday I sketched the life of Josephus, dwelling more particularly on his activities as commander in the opening campaign in Galilee, and then as mediator during the siege of Jerusalem. To-day the scene shifts from Palestine to Rome, from the battlefield to the historian's study and the opening of his literary career with the most famous of his works, the *History of the Jewish War*. The first-fruits of the leisure which he found in Rome after the campaign, it was written with all the advantages possessed by an ex-combatant and eyewitness, now a pensioner quartered in peace and comfort in the former palace of Vespasian, with his own memoranda at hand and Roman official records of the war placed at his disposal. What use did he make of his materials? What were his motives and purpose? How far is the credibility of the narrative affected by the personality of its author and his relation to his patrons, or by conformation to certain contemporary conventional methods of writing history? Those are among the questions to be considered.

The author has in three of his writings told us a good deal about the origin of this work and the manner of its composition, and it will be well to begin with his actual words, and then see what deductions can be drawn from them.

His proem to the work opens with a reference to the magnitude of the war of the Jews against the Romans and the inadequacy of previous histories of it. Of these earlier historians, he says,[1] " some, having taken no part in the action, have collected from hearsay

[1] *B.J.* i. 1–3.

casual and contradictory stories, which they have then edited in a rhetorical style; while others, who witnessed the events, have, either from flattery of the Romans or from hatred of the Jews, misrepresented the facts, their writings exhibiting alternately invective and encomium, but nowhere historical accuracy. In these circumstances, I—Josephus, son of Matthias, a Hebrew by race, a native of Jerusalem and a priest, who at the opening of the war myself fought against the Romans and in the sequel was perforce an onlooker—propose to provide the subjects of the Roman Empire with a narrative of the facts, by translating into Greek the account which I previously composed in my vernacular tongue and sent to the up-country barbarians." He is now writing for an educated Greek-speaking public, and "barbarians" means simply "non-Hellenic"; a little lower down he specifies more precisely who are these "barbarians in the interior," these "backwoodsmen," as we may say. "I thought it monstrous," he writes,[2] "to allow the truth in such matters to go astray, and that, while Parthians and Babylonians and the most remote tribes of Arabia, along with our countrymen beyond the Euphrates and the inhabitants of Adiabene[3] were, through my assiduity, accurately acquainted with the origin of the war, the various phases of calamity through which it passed and its conclusion, the Greeks and such Romans as were not engaged in the contest should remain in ignorance of these matters, with flattering or fictitious narratives as their only guide." From these statements we learn not only that widespread interest in the war had already caused a considerable output of previous histories, but that our author's extant Greek work had been preceded by an earlier Semitic[3a] draft addressed to Eastern readers.

Some thirty years later, when his own work had come in for its share of criticism, he makes two further allusions to the circum-

[2] *B.J.* i. 6.

[3] In the upper Tigris region on the Parthian frontier. The dynasty of Adiabene had under Claudius been converted to Judaism and some members of the royal family fought on the side of the Jews in the war.   [3a] Whether Aramaic or Hebrew.

stances under which it was written. In the Autobiography he takes Justus of Tiberias to task for withholding his rival history, written twenty years before, until after the death of the last of the principal actors in the war, King Agrippa, and only publishing it when he thought he could no longer be confuted. He then proceeds: [4] "I had no such apprehensions concerning my work. No; I presented the volumes to the emperors themselves, when the events had hardly passed out of sight, conscious as I was that I had presented the true story. I expected to receive testimony to my accuracy, and was not disappointed. To many others also I immediately presented my *History*, some of whom had taken part in the war, such as King Agrippa and certain of his relatives. Indeed, so anxious was the emperor Titus that my volumes should be the sole authority from which the world should learn the facts, that he affixed his own signature to them and gave orders for their publication; while King Agrippa wrote 62 letters testifying to the truth of the record." He appends two specimens of these royal epistles. The first, ending "Send me the remaining volumes," shows that the work appeared in parts. The second, obviously a hasty scrawl in slipshod Greek, runs: "King Agrippa to dearest Josephus, greeting. From what you have written you appear to stand in no need of instruction, to enable us all (ἡμᾶς ὅλους) to learn (everything from you) from the beginning. But when you meet me, I will myself inform you of much that is not generally known." "And," continues Josephus, "on the completion of my *History*, not in flattery, which was contrary to his nature, nor yet, as you (Justus) no doubt will say, in irony, for he was far above such malignity, but in all sincerity, he, in common with all readers of my volumes, bore witness to their accuracy."

In a third passage, in the *contra Apionem*,[5] he writes in much the same strain, adding some interesting details. Alluding, as in the proem already quoted, to other so called histories of the war put together from hearsay reports by persons who were nowhere

[4] *Vita* 361 ff.   [5] *Ap.* i. 46 ff.

near the scene of action, and to unnamed critics of his own work, doubtless meaning Justus, he writes: "I, on the contrary, have written a veracious account...having been present at all the events. I was in command of those whom we call Galilaeans, so long as resistance was possible; after my capture I was a prisoner in the Roman camp... Subsequently I was liberated and sent... with Titus to the siege of Jerusalem. During that time no incident escaped my knowledge. I kept a careful record of all that went on under my eyes in the Roman camp, and was alone in a position to understand the information brought by deserters. Then, in the leisure which Rome afforded me, with all my materials in readiness, and with the aid of some assistants for the sake of the Greek, at last I committed to writing my narrative of the events. So confident was I of its veracity that I presumed to take as my witnesses, before all others, the commanders-in-chief in the war, Vespasian and Titus. They were the first to whom I presented my volumes, copies being afterwards given to many Romans who had taken part in the campaign. Others I *sold* to a large number of my compatriots, persons well versed in Greek learning, among whom were Julius Archelaus,[6] the most venerable Herod [7] and the most admirable King Agrippa himself.[8] All these bore testimony to my scrupulous safeguarding of the truth, and they were not the men to conceal their sentiments or keep silence had I, through ignorance or partiality, distorted or omitted any of the facts. And yet certain despicable persons have essayed to malign my history, regarding it as a prize composition such as is set to boys at school," and so on. Here there are several points of interest. There is the belated acknowledgment of assistance in the Greek. There is the criticism in the last sentence which has evidently wounded our author. It is not, I think, an imputation of crudity of style, of which, thanks to the author's able assistants, the work cannot be accused, but on the contrary that he has sacrificed accuracy to brilliance. The

[6] Son of Chelcias and husband of Mariamme, sister of Agrippa II.
[7] Unidentified.   [8] Agrippa II.

unnamed critic is contrasting Josephus with the great Athenian historian, who, careless whether his sober narrative, devoid of myth (τὸ μὴ μυθῶδες) should be disappointing to the ear, remarks in a famous phrase, " My history is an everlasting possession, not a prize composition which is heard and forgotten." [9] Lastly, we see our author acting as his own bookseller. In the *Life* we are told that King Agrippa received a presentation copy, here that he was one of the purchasers. I suppose we may conclude that the pleasure derived from the first copy induced him to buy a second.

From these statements two main facts emerge. First, the work was written under Roman auspices. It received the *imprimatur* of Titus: its accuracy was vouched for not only by the Roman commanders, but by various members of the tributary royal house, in particular King Agrippa, who was consulted at every stage of its composition. Secondly, it was issued in two forms, an earlier probably Aramaic draft for eastern readers, followed by a Greek edition for the western world.

Putting these two facts together, and noting the priority given to the edition intended for the East and the rapidity with which it must have been composed and circulated, we can safely, I think, draw one inference, as to the motive of the work, already acutely detected by Herr Laqueur [10]: Josephus was commissioned by the conquerors to write the official history of the war for propagandist purposes. It was a manifesto, intended as a warning to the East of the futility of further opposition and to allay the after-war thirst for revenge, which ultimately found vent in the fierce outbreaks under Trajan and Hadrian. A glance at the list of contemplated readers in the proem [11] is suggestive: " Parthians and Babylonians and the most remote tribes of Arabia with our countrymen beyond the Euphrates and the inhabitants of Adiabene."

[9] *Thuc.* i. 22 (Jowett).
[10] Laqueur, *Der jüd. Historiker* 126 f., 255.
[11] *B.J.* i. 6.

The danger of a Parthian rising was a constant menace to Rome, and the placing of that race in the forefront is significant. Again, great hopes had been built by the Palestinian Jews in the recent war on assistance from their brethren in Babylon. "The whole of the Eastern Empire," writes Josephus,[12] "was in the balance; the insurgents were fired with hopes of its acquisition, their opponents feared its loss. For the Jews hoped that all their brethren beyond the Euphrates would join with them in revolt." These expectations were at the time frustrated; but in the later revolt under Trajan the Diaspora in Mesopotamia played a leading part.[13] With the list of readers mentioned in the proem should be compared the speech which is put into the mouth of Agrippa before hostilities began, where the same names recur:[14] "What allies then do you expect for this war?... For in the habitable world all are Romans—unless, may be, the hopes of some of you soar beyond the Euphrates and you count on obtaining aid from your kinsmen in Adiabene. But they will not, on any frivolous pretext, let themselves be embroiled in so serious a war, and, if they did contemplate such folly, the Parthian would not permit it; for he is careful to maintain the truce with the Romans and would regard it as a violation of the treaty if any of his tributaries were to march against them." Adiabene was the region east of the Tigris on the Parthian frontier. Its pious queen Helena and her sons were notable converts to Judaism, as the Jews always proudly recalled, and, notwithstanding Agrippa's alleged words, some members of the royal family actually fought on their side.

This pacific or propagandist motive, which may safely be inferred from such passages, is in fact explicitly avowed by the author in the remark with which he closes his classical description of the Roman army: "If I have dwelt at some length on this topic," he writes,[15] "my intention was not so much to extol the Romans as

---

[12] *ib.* 4 f.

[13] Mommsen, *Provinces* ii. 221 f.

[14] *B.J.* ii. 388 f.   [15] *B.J.* iii. 108.

to console those whom they have vanquished and *to deter others who may be tempted to revolt.*"

Thus Josephus, who had been employed by Titus throughout the siege to counsel submission by oral exhortation, was now again employed by the conquerors to deter his compatriots from further revolt by his pen. He was to serve their interest, indeed, but also to serve his own country. He was no mere hireling; his own deepest convictions told him that the only road to amelioration [16] of his nation's unhappy lot lay in submission to the empire. How far his narrative may have been distorted by pro-Roman bias is another matter, which remains to be considered. But of the sanity of his counsels there can be no doubt: the verdict of history—the culminating disasters under Hadrian—showed that, at least from the standpoint of worldly wisdom, he was right.

The original Aramaic edition was lost at an early date, being superseded by the Greek work addressed to the Western world. Of the theory recently advanced that the Aramaic may have survived in the old Russian version I will speak immediately; but it will be convenient first to refer to another matter which may have a bearing on the lost work—I mean the titles. The book has come down to us with two distinct titles. Are we justified in connecting these two titles with the two drafts, Aramaic and Greek?

The title by which the book is ordinarily known is " (Concerning) the Jewish War," Greek Περὶ τοῦ Ἰουδαϊκοῦ πολέμου, Latin *De bello Judaico*. And that is in fact the name by which the author refers to it in his later writings.[17] Once more we are indebted to

---

[16] *Cf. B. J.* v. 19.

[17] *Ant.* i. 203 " as I have previously stated when writing the *Jewish War*," xviii. 11 " We have spoken about them (the three Jewish sects) in the second book of the *Jewish War*," xx. 258 " (all that we did and endured) can be learnt in detail by any who will peruse the books which I wrote on the Jewish War," *Vita* 412 "... all that I did in the Jewish War and at the siege of Jerusalem I have narrated in detail in my books concerning the Jewish War."

the acute German critic, Herr Laqueur,[18] for pointing out that this name originated in Roman circles: so entitled, the book announces on its face that it is written from the Roman standpoint. For Ἰουδαϊκὸς πόλεμος means not "The war of the Jews," but "the war against the Jews." The insurgents would speak of the Roman war or, more fully, the war of the Jews against the Romans: they would never use the simple gentilic adjective "Jewish." Caesar's *De bello Gallico* forms an exact analogy, or, to take a modern example, "the South African war": neither Gauls nor Boers would so describe those contests. We must assume that in Rome Josephus accommodated himself to Roman habit: "Jewish War" was the name by which his Roman customers were accustomed to order a copy of his work. But it seems incredible that the author, desiring to catch the ear of eastern readers and to deter them from further revolution by his narrative of the recent struggle, should have defeated his own object by prefixing a title that must have sounded so offensive, doubly offensive if coupled with his Roman name, Flavius Josephus. Moreover, though the author had evidently contracted the habit in Rome of speaking of his "Jewish War" and indeed only mentions it under that name, that title appears in none of our MSS. Only in the inscription to the first two books in Niese's principal MS (P) do we find a modified form of it, "(a history) of the Jewish War against the Romans" (Ἰουδαϊκοῦ πολέμου πρὸς Ῥωμαίους). Here the added words seem intended to remove the objectionableness of the shorter title; but correction has not been carried far enough, for the adjective "Jewish" i. e. "against the Jews" remains, and, as Laqueur remarks, we have a double mention of the opponents.

On the other hand, all the rest of Niese's MSS, including P in the later books, employ another title "concerning (the) capture" (περὶ ἁλώσεως), to which is usually prefixed or appended "of Jewish history" (Ἰουδαϊκῆς ἱστορίας). This title recurs in other writers, such as Origen and Jerome, the latter of whom attributes

[18] *Der jüd. Historiker* 98, cf. 255.

it to the author himself: "quae Josephus Judaicae scriptor historiae septem explicat voluminibus, quibus imposuit titulum Captivitatis Judaicae id est περὶ ἁλώσεως." [19] Internal evidence supports the ascription of this title to the author. The word ἅλωσις is constantly used by him of the final tragedy, in connexion with the cardinal events that led up to it. Thus the massacre of the Roman garrison "seemed to the Jews like the prelude to capture (or ruin)" (προοίμιον ἁλώσεως, ii. 454): again he writes, "I should not be wrong in saying that the capture of the city began with the death of Ananus" (iv. 318), and again he calls "the Zealots' attack on the populace the first step towards the city's capture" (v. 3). This quasi-technical use of the word in the work itself, together with the evidence of Jerome and the almost unanimous evidence of the MSS, convinces me that this (περὶ ἁλώσεως) is the older title, and not improbably a survival of the Semitic title of the lost Aramaic edition. I have been gradually converted to the opinion of my friend Dr. Robert Eisler, who draws a distinction between an older and simpler Greek draft, the *Halosis*, and a later and more elaborate edition, the *Polemos* or "Jewish War." The *Halosis*, in his view, was perhaps issued in time for the imperial triumph in 71 A.D. This early form of the work was gradually revised, curtailed in some places, expanded in others, in subsequent years; the *Jewish War* was the title of the final edition published during the reign of Domitian.

And now I must briefly refer to the theory that the original Aramaic draft has survived in a Russian dress. I cannot do more than touch on this large and contentious question, more especially as the materials are not yet fully accessible to scholars and I have not had the opportunity for a thorough study of those which have already been published. Full information is to be looked for in the important forthcoming work of Dr. Robert Eisler, by whose masterly investigation of the subject I have been deeply influenced.

[19] Comm. in Isaiam cap. 64 *sub fin.*

In 1906, in Harnack's well-known series of *Texte und Unter-suchungen*,[20] the late Dr. Berendts published a German version of some extracts from a North Slavonic or old Russian Josephus. These extracts consisted of some very extraordinary statements relating to John the Baptist, anonymously referred to as "the savage," Jesus also unnamed and called "the wonder-worker," and the early Christians. These passages find no parallel in our Greek MSS of the *War*, which make no allusion to Christianity or to its Founder or His forerunner. The 17 known Russian MSS are not earlier than the 15th century; the actual translation goes back two centuries earlier, to about 1250 A.D. Perhaps the most important part of Dr. Eisler's work is that in which he has traced the origin of the Slavonic Josephus back to a Judaizing heresy which in the middle of the 13th century invaded Russia and even for a while the court of the Tsar. The MSS from which the version was made were doubtless obtained from Constantinople. Berendts put forward the theory that these strange allusions to Christianity were the genuine work of Josephus, relics of the original Aramaic draft of the *War*, which were afterwards suppressed. Berendts' theory met with little support at the time: it was ridiculed by Schürer and other critics. But no satisfactory explanation of these mysterious passages was offered, or was possible pending the publication of a complete text. Before his death Dr. Berendts had prepared a German version of the first four books of the Slavonic text, and this has now been edited by Professor Grass of Dorpat.[21] The last three books still await a translator, but, through the liberality of Dr. James Loeb, Dr. Eisler has been able to obtain complete photographs, which I understand will ultimately find a home in this country, and ere long we may hope that the whole work will be accessible in an intelligible tongue.

20 N.F. Bd. xiv.

21 *Flavius Josephus vom Jüdischen Kriege, Buch i–iv, nach der slavischen Übersetzung deutsch herausgegeben* ... von A. Berendts und K. Grass, Dorpat, Teil I 1924–26, Teil II 1927.

That the Slavonic is *directly* derived from the lost Aramaic cannot be maintained, as Berendts himself recognised. Investigation of his German version soon reveals that the Slavonic is a translation from *Greek*, and from a MS which, though differing from all known Greek MSS, had affinities to a particular group of MSS which Niese regarded as "inferior" and did not adopt as the basis of his text. That is not, however, so serious an objection to the originality of the Slavonic and of the underlying Greek exemplar as might at first sight appear. The two types of Greek text can be traced back to the 3rd century and may conceivably both go back to the author himself, who constantly revised his writings. The "inferiority" of the readings of the MSS in question (VRC) may be due to their having preserved an original rougher draft, which the author improved in later editions. Dr. Eisler's opinion is that the Slavonic is a translation from Josephus' first rough Greek version of the original Aramaic, before it was rewritten in the form in which it has come down to us. That is the conclusion to which some of the evidence seems to point. Below the Greek Dr. Eisler finds, in certain transliterated words, indications of an underlying Semitic original. The style is simpler than the extant Greek: in particular direct speech (*oratio recta*) constantly replaces indirect. The text is shorter. The proem, with its criticism of Greek historians, is, as might be expected, absent, though the long introductory narrative from the time of Antiochus Epiphanes is included. The simple style and the shorter text may in part be attributed to the Slavonic translator, who clearly often failed to understand his Greek original; but deliberate abbreviation will not wholly account for the absence of some of the longer or mutually connected sections. It is, however, the additional matter in the Slavonic which has aroused most interest. Of the allusions to Christianity I will speak in a later lecture. But there are other passages, such as descriptions of dreams (a favourite topic of Josephus), a priestly debate about Herod's claims to the throne and the expected Messiah, the ruse by which Josephus escaped with his life in the cave at Jotapata, which are difficult to explain except as the productions of the Jewish historian, which for various reasons have been suppressed. Until other explanation of such passages is forthcoming I should therefore tentatively regard the Slavonic as representing, not a verbatim reproduction of the original Aramaic, but an intermediate stage between it and the extant Greek.

From the lost Aramaic, perhaps partially preserved in this old Russian, I turn to the extant Greek text. This, though described by the author as a translation from the Aramaic, in fact shows no trace of Semitic parentage. The style of the whole work is an excellent specimen of the Atticistic Greek fashionable in the first century. Either the translator has done his work extraordinarily well, or, as is far more probable, the older work has been practically rewritten. That Josephus uses the word "translate" loosely, we know from his other principal work. He describes his *Antiquities* as a translation from the Hebrew Scriptures;[22] but we know that in fact that work is a free paraphrase of the Biblical story, made with some assistance from the older LXX version, but in no sense a literal translation of his own or of others. Still the words used in the *War* (Ἑλλάδι γλώσσῃ μεταβαλών) would be more intelligible, if the polished version produced with the aid of collaborators had been preceded by a rougher draft such as we find in the Slavonic. We know that the author in later life, in A.D. 93–4, was contemplating a new edition of the *War*, which was to include the after events of his nation's history brought up to date.[23] He was constantly rewriting his work, and our extant Greek text is not necessarily the original form.

This brings me to the scope and limits of his work, and to the question of date. Here again, there are indications of growth, especially of additions at the end. The latest dated event mentioned is the dedication of the Temple of Peace,[24] with its world-famous museum of treasures, including some of the principal trophies from Jerusalem. This, as we know from Dio Cassius,[25] took place in

[22] *Ant.* i. 5, cf. x. 218.   [23] *Ant.* xx. 267.   [24] *B.J.* vii. 158 ff.   [25] lxvi. 15.

the year 75, and the publication of the *War* is commonly fixed as falling between 75 and 79, the year of the death of Vespasian who received a copy. These limits may, however, apply only to a single edition, and there is reason to think that the work was once shorter and that portions, at least of the last book, are later appendices. The story of the capture of Jerusalem is concluded in Book vi— a natural stopping point; Book vii comprises the triumphal procession and the aftermath of the war—the extermination of the last strongholds in Palestine, Machaerus and Masada, the rising of the Sicarii in Alexandria, the demolition of the temple of Onias in Egypt, and a final rising in Cyrene, in which the historian was accused of being implicated. Book vii as a whole is distinguished from the earlier books by its style; there is a large admixture of phraseology characteristic of the *Antiquities* and less indication of help from the author's able assistants. He seems to have been more dependent on his own resources. This evidence suggests that Book vii, in whole or in part, may have been added later.

Dr. Eisler, relying mainly on the different endings of the old Russian MSS, goes into greater detail, and reconstructs the various stages by which the work has reached its present form. The last event mentioned in the author's incomplete "table of contents" in his proem is the triumph. Dr. Eisler infers that the first Greek edition ended there, and appeared as early as A.D. 71, the author striving to complete a copy for presentation to the emperors on that memorable occasion. One Moscow MS ends after the troubles in Alexandria, omitting the demolition of the Onias temple and events in Cyrene: this marks a second stage (early in 73). Later in that year came the news of the closure of the Onias temple which had lasted, according to Josephus, for 343 years, actually for about a century less. With the addition of this appendix Dr. Eisler ingeniously connects the mention of the foundation of this temple at the beginning of Book i,[26] now, according to him, prefixed for the first time. He now read the meaning of the divine chastisement,

[26] *B.J.* i. 33.

which was due to the existence of this second schismatic temple in defiance of the Deuteronomic law, and reshaped his history accordingly. This clever theory would account for the pre-war history being carried right back to the time of Antiochus Epiphanes, nearly 2½ centuries before the outbreak of the Roman war; but it has to be admitted that it lacks external support. Lastly, other Russian MSS stop short in the middle of the troubles in Cyrene, omitting the accusation brought against Josephus of being implicated in the plot. The Russian translator seems to have employed more than one Greek MS; but the inference drawn by Dr. Eisler from these various endings of the Russian MSS that they are derived from older and shorter forms of the work seems a little precarious.

I pass from the genesis of the work and the stages in its composition to the *materials* from which it has been constructed. Throughout his later and larger work, the *Antiquities*, the author intersperses constant allusions to his authorities. No similar allusions are to be found in the *Jewish War*. The historian in his earlier work is consistently and, it would seem, deliberately silent as to his sources, merely leading us to infer from his proem that his information is largely first-hand and based on his own recollections as an eyewitness, that he is independent of previous historians, has collected the facts with laborious care and constructed the framework of the narrative himself. Contrasting himself with the erudite Greeks who neglect the stirring actions of their own times and confine themselves to writing up the great historians of the past, he remarks: "The industrious writer is not one who merely remodels the scheme and arrangement of another's work, but one who tells of recent events and makes the framework of the history his own." [27]

---

[27] *B.J.* i. 15 φιλόπονος... ὁ μετὰ τοῦ καινὰ λέγειν καὶ τὸ σῶμα τῆς ἱστορίας κατασκευάζων ἴδιον. This recalls the attack on Justus, who claimed credit for industrious research (ὑπὲρ τοῦ δοκεῖν φιλόπονος εἶναι) in *Vita* 338; but, though wanting in the Slavonic, the proem to the *War* can hardly be brought down so late as the second century, when Justus' work appeared.

These scanty hints can be supplemented by some notices, already mentioned, in his later works—references to the notes which he kept throughout the siege of proceedings in the Roman camp, to the information as to the condition of affairs within the city supplied by deserters, and to the long correspondence with Agrippa.

Notwithstanding the emphasis laid on the author's personal contributions as eyewitness and reporter, it is probable that, apart from the early Galilaean campaign and a few other scenes in which he plays a prominent part, his own notes and recollections are a comparatively minor factor in the narrative. The bulk of it appears to be derived from a documentary source of Roman origin. That is suggested, *inter alia*, by numerous close parallels to Josephus to be found in the other, unfortunately fragmentary, account of the opening scenes of the war contained in the 5th book of the *Histories* of Tacitus. These *Histories* were written at Rome almost within the lifetime of Josephus, but the Roman's antipathy to the Jews makes it improbable that he consulted our author's work. Both seem to be dependent on a common source. What was that document?

Wilhelm Weber, in a recent suggestive book,[28] maintains that the backbone of the whole narrative is a " Flavian work," of which the theme was the rise to power of the Flavian dynasty. This opened with a sketch of the disposition of the Roman legions in A.D. 66 (incorporated in the great speech which Josephus puts into the mouth of Agrippa), included the bulk of Books iii–vi, and ended with the triumph when, in the words of Josephus, " the city of Rome kept festival at once for her victory in the campaign against her enemies, for the termination of her civil dissensions, and for her dawning hopes of felicity." To this theory it has been justly objected that the scathing reference which Josephus makes to previous publications on the war renders it highly improbable that he has based his narrative on a literary work of this nature.

[28] *Josephus und Vespasian*, Berlin, 1921.

The source is rather to be sought higher up, in fact at the fountain-head of intelligence from the Roman standpoint. The author appears to have had access to a document of the first importance, no less than the "memoirs" or "commentaries" (ὑπομνήματα) of the Roman commanders, Vespasian and Titus. No allusion is made to these *Commentaries* in the *War* itself, but they are thrice mentioned elsewhere in contexts which show that Josephus was familiar with them. In the autobiography, replying to the attacks of Justus of Tiberias, Josephus reminds him of certain hostilities for which he and his fellow-citizens were responsible at the opening of the war, and which were brought to the notice of Vespasian on his arrival. He adds:[29] "This is no unsupported assertion of my own. The facts are recorded in the *Commentaries* of the Emperor Vespasian, which further relate how the inhabitants of Decapolis pressed him, when at Ptolemais, to punish you as the culprit." Ptolemais was the point reached on the first march of Vespasian from his base at Antioch; the *Commentaries* therefore went back to the opening of the campaign. Further on, addressing the same opponent, Josephus writes:[30] "Perhaps, however, you will say that you have accurately narrated the events which took place at Jerusalem. How, pray, can that be, seeing that neither were you on the scene of action, nor had you perused the *Commentaries* of Caesar (i. e. Titus), as is abundantly proved by your account which conflicts with those *Commentaries*?" In other words, says our author, "You had not either of my advantages." Again, in the *contra Apionem*,[31] "Surely one cannot but regard as audacious the attempt of these critics to challenge my veracity. Even if, as they assert, they have read the *Commentaries* of the imperial commanders, they at any rate had no first-hand acquaintance with our position in the opposite camp." These two last passages in which the writer is contrasting his own qualifications with those of others, clearly imply that the *Commentaries* were before him when he wrote the *War*.

[29] *Vita* 342.   [30] *ib.* 358.   [31] *Ap.* i. 56.

The author's silence in the work itself concerning his main source is in keeping with contemporary custom and intelligible on other grounds. As Professor Cadbury has pointed out in a recent work,[32] it was the common practice of historians to use sources without naming them and to name sources without using them. The main source was unnamed, its language being not retained *verbatim*, but paraphrased and transformed into the style of the author who used it. On the other hand, a subsidiary source, which the writer did not follow, might be named in occasional instances of a conflict of authorities: there are many instances of that in our author's *Jewish Antiquities*. In the *War* there was apparently but the one main document, and that remains nameless. Josephus was thus only doing as others did in concealing this Roman source of information. But perhaps without injustice his silence may partly be attributed to vanity. He would have us know that the framework of the narrative is his own, and a mention of this source, whatever weight it might add to his authority, might detract from his personal fame, and indeed from his claim to impartiality. At any rate, like his acknowledgment of aid from his Greek assistants, his allusions to the *Commentaries* only appear in his later works, where they are evoked by the criticisms of Justus and others.

The *Commentarii principales* were, we may suppose, the daily record of military proceedings, based on the notes, presumably in Latin, made on the field of action by the Roman commanders and their staff. These rough materials might be subsequently put out in a more literary shape by the commander himself as the official record of the campaign, like the *Commentarii de Bello Gallico* of Julius Caesar; more often the working up of the polished narrative would be left to professional hands. The original language of the underlying record is, like the original Aramaic of our author's first draft, overlaid and almost concealed, but occasionally the Latin still shines through. Thus, when we read that the Romans' incentives to valour were "their continuous campaigns and perpetual training, the magnitude of their empire, and above all Titus, ever and everywhere present beside all (Τίτος ἀεὶ πᾶσιν πανταχοῦ παρατυγχάνων),[33] the collocation of " ever, everywhere, all " strongly suggests that Latin phrase " quod semper, quod ubique, quod ab omnibus," familiar as a definition of the Christian Catholic faith, but for which older pagan parallels can be found. To this source we may, *inter alia,* attribute the concise itinerary of the march of Titus from Alexandria to Caesarea, with its bare enumeration of the various stages,[34] the names and occasionally descriptions [35] of the Roman heroes who distinguished themselves in the various engagements, even perhaps some of the geographical sketches of Palestine interspersed throughout the narrative, such as the description of the Dead Sea to which Vespasian paid a visit of exploration: [36] the account in Tacitus [37] offers some striking parallels and is probably derived from the same source. From this or from some other official source must come the information with regard to the disposition of the Roman legions throughout the provinces of the Roman empire on the outbreak of the war in A.D. 66, here worked up into the great speech of King Agrippa,[38] and strikingly confirmed by other evidence. References to the Jewish enemy as "*the* nation" (not "our nation") or "the barbarians" also betray the hand of a foreigner.

For the pre-war period, the long introductory history which fills the first and the bulk of the second book, Josephus is again apparently dependent in the main on a single writer, here unnamed, but frequently mentioned in the *Antiquities*, Nicolas of Damascus, the intimate friend of Herod the Great and of the emperor Augustus, author of a universal history and other works, including perhaps a separate life of Herod. Nicolas is probably the authority for the slight opening sketch of the Hasmonaean house ; the historian here shows no certain acquaintance with the first book of Maccabees,

[33] *B.J.* v. 310.   [34] *ib.* iv. 658–end.
[35] *ib.* vi. 54 f., Sabinus: " his skin was black, his flesh shrunk and emaciated."
[36] *ib.* iv. 476 ff.   [37] *Hist.* v. 6.   [38] *B.J.* ii. 345 ff.

of which he afterwards made large use in the *Antiquities*. From
Nicolas undoubtedly comes the disproportionately detailed story
of Herod the Great, which fills two-thirds of Book i, and of the
accession of Archelaus, in which he himself played a leading part
as advocate of the heir to the throne.

For the sixty years intervening between Archelaus and the outbreak of the war Josephus might be expected to have obtained information on Agrippa I from that monarch's son, his friend
Agrippa II, and for later events to have drawn upon his own
recollections; but Dr. Eisler has acutely shown that he is mainly
dependent for this period on official documents preserved in Rome.

Besides the materials accessible to the historian, another factor
in the composition of his work, of which account must be taken
in estimating its character and credibility, is its conformity to certain
current conventions of its age.   One recognised convention among
ancient historians was the insertion into the narrative of speeches
put into the mouths of the leading characters.[39] Josephus freely
indulges in this practice, and a few words may be said about his
speeches.   These orations were a licensed field for invention and
the display of rhetorical skill, subject to some minor restrictions,
of which the need for a shorthand reporter was not one.   "Like the
chorus in a Greek play," as Professor Cadbury writes, "they served
to review the situation for the reader, and they brought out the
inner thoughts and feelings of important persons."   The example
had been set by the sober Thucydides, whose speeches are world-
famous, and who did make some effort to recover the actual words.
You will remember his classic allusion to the subject: "As to the
speeches which were made either before or during the war, it was
hard for me, and for others who reported them to me, to recollect
the exact words.   I have therefore put into the mouth of each
speaker the sentiments proper to the occasion, expressed as I thought
he would be likely to express them, while at the same time I

[39] In this and the following I am indebted to Cadbury, *Making of Luke-Acts* 184 ff.

endeavoured, as nearly as I could, to give the general purport of
what was actually said." [40]   Later writers were not so scrupulous
and nothing more was required than that the speeches should be
" in character."   Speeches may be either direct or indirect, the
latter form probably more nearly approaching the authentic address
than the other.   Julius Caesar in his *De Bello Gallico* almost
invariably reports his own speeches in *oratio indirecta*.[41]   Direct
speech, on the other hand, was the usual medium for oratorical
display and the expression of the historian's views.

In Josephus the speeches may roughly be divided into three classes.
A small minority perhaps approximate to the words actually spoken.
Speeches arising out of a particular occasion, especially exhortations
to troops before or after battle, form an intermediate group: these
are in keeping with the character of the speaker and, where he is
one of the historian's imperial patrons, Vespasian or Titus, may
preserve the gist of what was said.   Lastly, we have the great " set "
speeches inserted at cardinal turning-points in the narrative: these
are purely imaginary and serve the purpose of propaganda.

An instance of a speech that probably approximates to the reality
is that of Nicolas of Damascus advocating the claims of Archelaus
to the succession to the Jewish throne before Augustus in Rome.
Josephus is here drawing either from the speaker's own report or
possibly from the imperial *acta*, to which also he had access, and
in which précis of the speeches delivered on that occasion would be
preserved.   The speech is twice reported, in *oratio obliqua*, in the
War and in the *Antiquities*; there are verbal variations, but the
tenor is the same.

The battle speeches of the Roman commanders preserve a
distinction between the character of Vespasian, the soldier grown
grey in the service with the steadiness of years and experience, and
the more impetuous Titus whose ripe manhood acts as the arm of
his father's brain.[42]   Twice over we find put into the mouth of

---

[40] *Thuc.* i. 22 (Jowett).   [41] Weber, *Josephus und Vespasian* 219.
[42] *Cf.* the description in *B.J.* iii. 4–6.

Titus what appears to be a reminiscence of a line in the *Electra* of Sophocles (ὅρα πόνου τοι χωρὶς οὐδὲν εὐτυχεῖ).[43] Before the walls of Tarichaeae Titus says to his troops, "But besides haste we need toil and resolution: great successes never come without risks":[44] and before Jerusalem "If any considered this an arduous operation, let him reflect that without toil nothing great could lightly be achieved by any man."[45] A commonplace, no doubt, but the Greek suggests a paraphrase of the Athenian poet. Titus, as we learn from Suetonius,[46] was "ready with Latin or Greek, whether in speaking or in composing poems." The reminiscence might therefore actually come from him, though it is more likely to be a delicate compliment of the historian or his amanuensis. Besides these battle speeches of the Roman generals, we have an exhortation of Herod the Great to his disconsolate troops after a defeat by the Arabs, followed by an earthquake. This is twice reported, in the *War*[47] and in the *Antiquities*,[48] and in totally different language. The speech in the *War* is Thucydidean, recalling that of Pericles to the Athenians exasperated by invasion and the plague:[49] the earthquake is here a "visitation of heaven" as the plague is there. In the *Antiquities* the only item which the speech has in common with that reported in the *War* is an allusion to the Arabs' crime in murdering Jewish envoys. The discrepancies indicate that both speeches are wholly imaginary.

But it is the elaborate set speeches for great occasions which are most significant. These are oratorical displays, subserving the general propagandist purpose of the work. "Bow to the invincible world empire," "It is the decree of destiny," that is their theme, and it is put into the mouths of the Jewish leaders, who must themselves be made to pronounce their impotence and righteous doom. We have three or more such speeches, that of Agrippa dissuading his countrymen from hostilities before the outbreak, that of Josephus

---

[43] Line 945.   [44] *B.J.* iii. 495.   [45] *ib.* v. 501.
[46] *Tit.* 3 "Latine Graeceque vel in orando vel in fingendis poematibus, promptus."
[47] *B.J.* i. 373–379.   [48] *Ant.* xv. 127–146.   [49] *Thuc.* ii. 60 ff.

beneath the walls of the beleaguered city, and that of the last outstanding rebel, Eleazar, at the close.

The great speech of Agrippa is a wonderful *tour de force*, and, though it was certainly never spoken, possesses distinct historical value, being comparable to the classical digression on the Roman army in the third book.[50] As you will remember, it is a survey of the Roman empire, province by province, and giving in each case the number of legions which suffice to maintain order. It has set the modern critic a problem to discover whether the distribution of the legions here set forth is that of the year 66, in which the speech purports to have been delivered, or, as seems more probable, of a rather later year. Dr. Eisler infers from some discrepancies in the Slavonic text that our author's older draft, the *Halosis*, did in fact represent the position in 66, that the particulars may have been obtained through Agrippa, who was attached to Vespasian's headquarters as leader of his auxiliary contingent, and that in the *War* we have the situation brought up to date in 75. In any case we may be sure on the one hand that the information is based on official records, on the other that Agrippa never delivered it. His short appended speech, in effect "Pay your tribute and restore the porticoes communicating with the Roman garrison in Antonia,"[51] may be genuine; but the writer of the slipshod letters preserved by the historian was hardly capable of such an oratorical effort.

From Josephus himself before the walls of Jerusalem we have a two-fold [52] speech counselling surrender, the first half in *oratio obliqua* on the theme "God is on the Roman side" and containing one fine phrase, "Fortune had from all quarters passed over to them, and God who went the round of the nations, bringing to each in turn the rod of empire, now rested over Italy," [53] the second half in *oratio recta* drawing from a survey of Jewish relations with foreign nations the lesson of history "Arms have not been granted to the Jews." Both portions were doubtless penned in the writer's

[50] *B.J.* ii. 345 ff., iii. 70 ff.   [51] *B.J.* ii. 403 f.
[52] *ib.* v. 362-374: 376-419.   [53] v. 367.

scriptorium in Rome, the former half in the more difficult *oratio indirecta* with able assistance.

At the close we have put into the mouth of one of the principal rebels, Eleazar, defender of the last stronghold of Masada now reduced to extremities, another double speech recommending the occupants of the fortress to destroy each other rather than submit to Rome. Here the theme is "God has sentenced us to destruction: the Romans cannot claim the credit of victory," and this is supported by an array of instances of recent Jewish disasters, for which Romans were not responsible. It is grimly entertaining to contrast the arguments here adduced in favour of self-destruction with those brought forward by Josephus himself to prove the iniquity of suicide when his own life was at stake at Jotapata.[54] He was a skilful advocate.

It remains for me to attempt to form some estimate of the general trustworthiness of the narrative. Materials, motive, personality— those are the principal factors that go to the making of a work of literature and determine its character and value; and from those points of view the credibility of the history of the *Jewish War* must be judged.

Of first-hand materials he had no lack. Rarely can war historian in ancient or modern times have enjoyed such a combination of opportunities for presenting a veracious picture of events. Combatant at the outset and then onlooker from the opposite camp, he had his own notes taken on the spot; he had access to the official record of the campaign compiled by, or under the supervision of, the enemy's generals—the *Commentaries* of Vespasian and Titus; for further information on matters "not generally known" he could apply to the Jewish King Agrippa, as he did in a prolonged correspondence; for particulars of events in Jerusalem and the horrors of the siege he had the evidence of deserters, whom he alone was in a position to understand. He had the perhaps more

[54] iii. 362–382.

questionable benefit of excellent literary assistants. General and historian like Thucydides, he shared with the great Athenian the advantage of viewing the campaign from the standpoint of both belligerents. "Associating with both sides, with the Peloponnesians quite as much as with the Athenians, because of my exile," writes Thucydides:[55] "I who at the opening of the war myself fought against the Romans and in the sequel was perforce an onlooker," writes Josephus.[56]

If we ask what use our historian made of these ample and first-hand materials and turn to consider his motives and personality, it must be confessed that his work cannot stand the test of comparison with that highest of standards, the *History of the Peloponnesian War*. Josephus lacks the sober impartiality of Thucydides and, with all his reiterated protestations of his zeal for the truth, shows from time to time, when his statements are subject to control, a lax sense of the full meaning of that word.

His motive, as I have said, is clear. His work is propagandist: he writes, as he himself says, to console the vanquished with the thought of the invincible might of imperial Rome and to deter his countrymen and others from further revolt.[57] He who speaks of "the innate generosity of the Romans to those whom they had once subdued"[58] doubtless voices the boasted motto of the victors in the Virgilian line "parcere subjectis et debellare superbos."[59] Yet in this attitude he did not stand alone among his countrymen. The Essenes, under whose spell he came in earlier life, compelled their novices to swear, *inter alia*, to "keep faith with all men, especially with the powers that be, since no ruler attains his office save by the will of God."[60] In very similar language another Pharisee of the Pharisees had preached to his Christian converts in Rome, "Let every soul be in subjection to the higher powers: for there is no power but of God, and the powers that be are ordained of God."[61] Even Johanan ben Zakkai, that stalwart patriot who

---

[55] *Thuc.* v. 26.   [56] *B.J.* i. 3.   [57] *ib*. iii. 108.   [58] *ib*. iii. 347.
[59] *Aen.* vi. 853.   [60] *B.J.* ii. 140.   [61] *Rom.* xiii. 1.

escaped from the beleaguered city in a coffin and who in the first difficult post-war days set out to recreate a new Judaism on the ruins of the past, a man of a very different stamp from Josephus, yet, like him, "is said to have predicted the calamitous outcome of the war, and during the siege of Jerusalem" to have "counselled peace with the Romans as the only salvation." [62] And there are other Rabbinical sayings to the same effect. It was probably in 66, at the time of the cessation of the daily sacrifices for Rome, an action which, as Josephus says, "laid the foundation of the war," [63] that R. Hanina uttered the warning, "Pray for the welfare of the government, for if it were not for the fear of it, men would swallow one another up alive"; and again, in the persecution under Hadrian, R. Jose ben Kisma preaches the same doctrine as Josephus, " This people (the Romans) has been given the kingdom by Heaven, for it has ruined his house, and burnt his temple, and slain his pious ones... and still it stands." [64] Josephus was thus not the mere puppet of the conquerors; he expresses his sincere convictions which were shared by other leaders of his race.

But I am concerned not so much with the question of the expediency of this policy and propagandist motive, as with its bearing on the truthfulness of the narrative. And here it must be confessed that the glamour of imperial Rome and adulation of his patrons have overcoloured the picture, detracted from the historian's impartiality and on occasion raised serious doubts as to his veracity. The campaign is viewed through Roman spectacles. The pro-Roman bias appears, as has been seen, on the very title page of the " Jewish War," in the speeches, in the panegyric on the Roman army (highly instructive as is that classic description), above all in the eulogy of the hero Titus. I have previously quoted the phrase about Titus " ever and everywhere present beside every-body," and we have numerous references to his personal and unaided

---

[62] Moore, *Judaism* ii. 116.

[63] *B.J.* ii. 409.

[64] *Abodah Zarah* 18 a, quoted with the previous passage by Moore, *op. cit.* ii. 114.

prowess. "Thus," writes Josephus in his account of a Jewish attack
on the Roman camp on the Mount of Olives before the siege, "thus,
if, without a syllable added in flattery or withheld from envy, the
truth must be told, Caesar personally twice rescued the entire legion
when in jeopardy, and enabled them to intrench themselves in their
camp unmolested." [65] But if this constant praise of his patron, that
magnetic personality who was not only the soldier's favourite but
was known as the "darling of the human race," [65a] is intelligible
and not wholly unmerited, we have one crucial instance where the
testimony of Josephus is directly contradicted by a later historian,
and his veracity is open to serious question. Josephus describes a
council of war upon the fate of the temple, at which, after the
expression of various opinions, Titus pronounced that it was under
all circumstances to be spared. The fourth-century Christian
writer, Sulpicius Severus, possibly dependent on the lost work of
Tacitus, also describes this council, but here the rôles are reversed
and it is Titus who sanctions the destruction of the building.[66] The
evidence of Sulpicius is vitiated by his putting into the mouth of
Titus some words about the Christians which can hardly be
authentic; but the known partiality of Josephus cannot but leave
him under the suspicion of misrepresenting the facts to clear his hero.

For the earlier pre-war history Josephus has afforded us a certain
check upon his statements and given us some insight into the
treatment of his sources by the duplicate narrative in his *Antiquities*.
The subject matter has been sometimes rearranged, the language has
been intentionally varied and there are not unnaturally some inconsistencies between the two accounts. But, generally speaking, it
may be said that the author faithfully follows his authorities, one
of whom, Nicolas, provides a vivid contemporary, if somewhat
biassed, picture of the monarch whose reign fills so large a place in
our author's earlier pages—Herod the Great.

[65] *B. J.* v. 97.   [65a] "deliciae generis humani" Suet. *Tit.* 1.

[66] *B. J.* vi. 238 ff., Sulpicius, *Chron.* ii. 30 ("At contra alii et Titus ipse evertendum
in primis templum censebant").

It is otherwise with the passages in which the *War* overlaps with the *Life*. Here, as I have said, there are unaccountable discrepancies, of a minor or graver character, which cannot all be attributed to carelessness. The author found himself in a difficult position in trying to reconcile his position as Jewish patriot and counsellor of peace with Rome. If we cannot penetrate to the true history of his early career in Galilee, there is here an obvious lack of candour, and these autobiographical notices must be pronounced untrustworthy. In some cases of inconsistency he has been suspected, not unjustly it would seem, of deliberate misrepresentation of details in order to ingratiate himself with his other patron, King Agrippa.

The narrative of the war is one-sided, and, to balance it and to see the other side of the picture, we would gladly recover the lost work of Justus of Tiberias, or, better still, have the story presented by Johanan ben Zakkai or by another of those who witnessed the siege from within. The villain, John of Gischala, cannot have been quite so black as he is here painted; and the "robbers" or Zealots would have another tale to tell of their patriotism. Josephus himself bears grudging testimony to the fortitude under persecution, comparable to that of the early Christian martyrs, of the Zealot refugees in Egypt, who refused under all manner of torture to acknowledge Caesar as their lord; [67] and the end of the devoted defenders of Masada was sublime.

But, after all reservations have been made, the narrative of our author in its main outlines must be accepted as trustworthy. Considered as a work of art, it takes high rank in literature; the reader's appreciation of its merits, for which the author is largely indebted to his skilled assistants and constant revision, grows on closer acquaintance. The poignant story is told with a pathos worthy of the theme and with all the resources of vivid and dramatic description. One specimen may fitly close this lecture. Many brilliant passages might be quoted: the rout of the legion of Cestius in the pass of Bethhoron, the burning of the Temple, the mutual

[67] *B.J.* vii. 417 ff.

destruction of the defenders of the last fortress of Masada. But
I will select one less tragic, in which the author himself figures,
and not without an element of humour—the reception at Jerusalem
of the news of the fall of Jotapata:— [68]

" When the news of the fate of Jotapata reached Jerusalem, it
was received at first with general incredulity, both because of the
magnitude of the calamity and because no eyewitness had come to
confirm the report. In fact, not a man had escaped to tell the tale;
rumour, with its natural propensity to black tidings, spontaneously
spread the news of the city's fall. Little by little, however, the
truth made its way from place to place, and was soon regarded by
all as established beyond doubt. But the facts were embroidered
by fiction; thus Josephus himself was reported to have fallen when
the city was taken. This intelligence filled Jerusalem with the
profoundest grief; whereas in each household and family there was
mourning of the relatives for their own lost ones, the lamentation
for the commander was national. While some mourned for a host,
others for a relative, some for a friend, others for a brother, all alike
wept for Josephus. Thus for thirty days the lamentations never
ceased in the city, and many of the mourners hired flute-players to
accompany their funeral dirges.

" But when time revealed the truth and all that had really
happened at Jotapata, when the death of Josephus was found to be
a fiction, and it became known that he was alive and in Roman
hands and being treated by the commanding officers with a respect
beyond the common lot of a prisoner, the demonstrations of wrath
at his being still alive were as loud as the former expressions of
affection when he was believed to be dead. Some abused him as a
coward, others as a traitor, and throughout the city there was general
indignation, and curses were heaped upon his devoted head."

Amid these imprecations of his countrymen, from which he was
thenceforth never to escape, I will leave the unfortunate historian
for this evening.

[68] *B. J.* iii. 432–439.

THE "JEWISH ANTIQUITIES"

I spoke yesterday of the most famous, and in many ways the finest, of our author's works, the *Jewish War*: to-day I turn to his *magnum opus*, the *Jewish Antiquities*, or, as we should rather call it by the Greek title which he used himself, the *Jewish Archaeology*. The two works in several respects present a marked contrast: in their rate of composition, the external conditions under which they were produced, and above all their motive. The *Jewish War* was written in the prime of life with surprising, almost lightning rapidity, one Aramaic edition and perhaps two in Greek appearing within half a dozen years of the campaign: the *Archaeology* was the laboured work of nearly twenty years of middle life, often apparently laid aside in weariness, and only finally carried to completion through the encouragement and instigation of others. The *War* was written with all the advantages of imperial patronage and support: the *Archaeology* was compiled under the last of the Flavians, a man of very different character from his father and brother—the emperor Domitian, the enemy of literature. Lastly, the earlier work was a message of warning addressed in the first instance to Jewish and eastern readers to deter them from further revolt by portraying the invincible majesty of Rome: the later was designed to magnify the Jewish race in the eyes of the Graeco-Roman world by a record of their ancient and glorious history.

The death of Titus in the year 81 and the accession of Domitian doubtless effected a change for the worse in the security of the

4*

historian's position. Laqueur [1] infers from an allusion in the auto-biography [2] to " Jewish accusers " that the occasion was seized by his opponents to represent Josephus to the new emperor as a traitor. By his usual tact the author succeeded in averting these dangers and retaining some share of imperial favour, but he had lost the active support of court in his literary undertakings. He was now writing under the blighting influence which in this reign deterred authorship of any description. We are told by Suetonius [3] that Domitian's reading was confined to the official reports of his grim predecessor Tiberius. Teuffel, the historian of Roman literature, writes: [4] " The superficial interest in literature, which Domitian had formerly dis-played vanished on his accession to the throne... (His) hand lay heavy on all intellectual life. Historical writing suffered most of all under his oppression... Under Domitian the only course possible without risk of outlawry or the sacrifice of personal honour, was the one followed by Juvenal, Tacitus and Pliny—namely, silence." It was, adds Teuffel, only the weak and servile who ventured to write, such as Martial and Josephus.

The collocation of these two authors is, however, a trifle unjust to Josephus, since he never refers to Domitian throughout the *Antiquities*, except once to date the year of its publication; [5] and the theme of this work was certainly not the glorification of Rome. On the contrary, deprived of his former patrons, he seems finally to sever his connexion with Roman political propaganda, and hence-forth figures solely as Jewish historian and apologist. But this severance of Roman ties and adoption of another and more patriotic theme do not, to my mind, indicate any abrupt change of attitude: Laqueur's suggestion [6] that in writing the *Antiquities* the author was prompted by self-interested motives, hoping to rehabilitate himself with his offended countrymen, seems to me fanciful. I do not doubt that the earlier work, with its counsel of submission to Rome, was

---

[1] *Der jüd. Historiker Fl. Josephus* 258.   [2] *Vita* 429.

[3] Suet., *Dom.* 20 " praeter commentarios et acta Tiberi Caesaris nihil lectitabat."

[4] *Hist. of Rom. Literature* ii. 109.   [5] *Ant.* xx. 267.   [6] *op. cit.* 260.

equally inspired by genuine patriotism, and we know that the project of writing his nation's history was no new one, having been conceived when he wrote the *Jewish War*.[7]

The author had lost or broken away from his old Roman friends. He was, it seems, also on less friendly terms, if he had not actually broken with his pro-Roman friend King Agrippa: that is suggested by a passage in the *Antiquities*[8] where he severely censures the crimes of Herod the Great, in opposition to his eulogist Nicolas, and regardless of hurting the feelings of his royal posterity. Bereft of his royal patrons, Josephus sought and found another in a certain Epaphroditus, to whom all his further writings are dedicated. The name was not uncommon, but this new friend is probably to be identified with Marcus Mettius Epaphroditus, a Greek grammarian mentioned by Suidas, who had been trained in Alexandria, and spent the latter part of his life in Rome, where he collected a library of 30,000 books and enjoyed a high reputation for learning, especially as a writer on Homer and the Greek poets. To him and his large library our author doubtless owes much of his learning, in particular that intimate acquaintance with Homeric problems and Greek mythology shown in the *contra Apionem*. In him too he found a publisher and advertiser of his writings.

From these external conditions under which the *Jewish Archaeology* was written, I pass to the author's *motives* and *models*, as set forth in an interesting proem to the work itself. He finds that historians are actuated by a variety of motives, of which he names four: an ostentation of skill in composition, flattery of the principal actors, personal participation in events impelling the eyewitness to narrate them, and the benefit to the public of a presentation of important and useful facts of which they are ignorant. He himself has been influenced by the two latter motives. His participation in and intimate knowledge of the events impelled him to write the *Jewish War*. His feeling that the Graeco-Roman world has much to learn from the history of his nation and will find it worthy of

[7] *Ant.* i. 6.   [8] *Ant.* xvi. 187.

study now constrains him to write the present *Archaeology*. He had in writing the earlier work contemplated prefixing such a history to it, but recognised that the scheme was too vast and decided to reserve the *Archaeology* for a separate work. Even so he has found the latter a very laborious task and has only been induced to carry it to completion by the instigation of his patron and other interested friends.

He had not lightly undertaken the work. Two questions had given him cause for serious reflection, concerning the propriety of such a work and the demand for it. On the one hand, he asked himself, Were our forefathers willing to impart such knowledge to others? on the other, Was there a Greek public anxious for the information? He found both questions satisfactorily answered in the traditional story of the origin of the Alexandrian version of the Scriptures. That enlightened monarch, Ptolemy Philadelphus, had keenly desired to add to his library a translation of the Jewish Law, and the high priest Eleazar had not grudged him every assistance, which he would certainly have refused had it been the custom of his nation to make a secret of its treasures. He, Josephus, would imitate Eleazar's generosity, in the belief that there were still many lovers of learning like-minded with the king; and, whereas that old Greek version had been limited to the Law, he would extend the narrative to the long and glorious record of the subsequent history. The work moreover would have a high moral purpose, viz. to show that true felicity comes only from following the revealed will of God, and to extol the merits of the lawgiver, who kept his narrative pure from the unseemly mythology current among others and had the most lofty conceptions of the Deity.

Such is the historian's preliminary statement, which calls for but little remark. On the question of publicity *versus* jealous reserve and obscurantism he sides with the Alexandrians. The legitimacy of paraphrasing the inspired Scriptures, especially in a foreign tongue, had always been a debatable point; and he doubtless has in mind the opinions of the contemporary Palestinian school of men like R. Johanan ben Zakkai and R. Akiba, now engaged at Jamnia in fixing the Hebrew text and building up a fence about the Law. Even at Alexandria, as Josephus would know from the *Letter of Aristeas*,[9] the perils of too free a use of Scripture were recognised. "How is it," says Philadelphus to his librarian, after hearing the reading of the Law, "that none of the historians or poets ever thought of mentioning such great deeds?," and he is told of the afflictions which befell Theopompus and Theodectes for their intention to introduce incidents from the Law into their works. But what was forbidden to the rash Gentile was lawful to the reverent Jew: the work of the Seventy had been followed up by the histories in more popular form of Demetrius and others, and one bold writer, Ezekiel, even ventured to present the story of the Exodus in the form of a Greek tragedy. In Palestine such undertakings were viewed with less friendly eyes. Even the Aramaic Targum had as yet hardly been committed to writing; and the Alexandrian version was now in disrepute. The alleged date of its production, observed at Alexandria as a festival, was kept by some Palestinians as a fast, and tradition asserted that the impious venture was punished by one of the old plagues of Egypt.[10] However, these objections have long since lost any validity which they may have ever possessed, and generations of readers are indebted to the Alexandrians, and still more to Josephus, for their knowledge of Jewish history. Incidentally it may be noted that while he correctly states that the original Greek version of the Scriptures was confined to the Law, he characteristically ignores the translation of the later books, of which he makes large use. As regards a reading public, the recent war had doubtless created a demand for such a work. The sculptures on the arch of Titus [11] would serve to arouse curiosity in Rome concerning the history of this ubiquitous

9 § 312 ff.

10 Appendix to *Megillath Ta'anith*, ed. Neubauer, *Anecdota Oxon.* Semitic Series, vol. i. pt. vi, Oxford 1895.

11 As Laqueur remarks, *op. cit.* 259.

race, whose religious influence was already making itself felt in every household.[12]

Josephus expressly names the Greek Bible as in a sense a model for his own work. But there was also another unacknowledged model, which would find even less favour in Palestinian circles, the Roman history of Dionysius of Halicarnassus. Such pagan models are kept in the background: neither Thucydides nor Dionysius is mentioned in our author's major works which derive much from them. Dionysius, an Asiatic, who like Josephus had migrated to the capital of the Empire, had in the year 7 ·B.C. produced in Greek a history of Rome, only second to that of Livy, entitled Ῥωμαϊκὴ Ἀρχαιολογία (*Roman Antiquities*) and comprised in 20 books. Exactly a century later Josephus produced his *magnum opus*, also in 20 books, to which he gave the title Ἰουδαϊκὴ Ἀρχαιολογία (*Jewish Antiquities*). There can be no doubt from the name and the identical number of books that this work is intended as a counterpart to the other. If, in his *Jewish War*, the author had offended Jewish susceptibilities by recommending submission to the conqueror, he would now make amends by showing that his race had a history comparable, nay in antiquity far superior, to that of the proud Roman. The work of Dionysius bore the name of *Archaeology*, being largely devoted to the earlier and mythical history of the race: Josephus would carry back his history, based on the Hebrew Scriptures, in which there was no admixture of "unseemly mythology current among others," to the creation of the world. Josephus was extolled by Jerome as "a second Livy": he might more aptly have been called "a second Dionysius." He owes nothing to Livy: of the influence of the Asiatic writer I will quote two further instances.

Here is our author's account of the passing of Moses:[13] "And while he embraced Eleazar and Joshua and was still talking with them, a cloud suddenly descended upon him and he disappeared in a ravine. But he has written of himself in the sacred books that he

[12] *c. Ap.* ii. 284.   [13] *Ant.* iv. 326.

died, for fear that men should venture to say that owing to his surpassing virtue he had gone back to the divinity." This seems clearly reminiscent of the passing of the two founders of the Roman race, Aeneas and Romulus, as described by Dionysius. "But the body of Aeneas," he writes,[14] "could nowhere be found and some conjectured that he had been translated to the gods"; and again of Romulus,[15] "The more mythical writers say that as he was holding an assembly[16] in the camp darkness descended upon him from a clear sky and... he disappeared, and they believe that he was caught up by his father Ares."

From Dionysius too, I think, is derived a recurrent formula, relating to incidents of a miraculous or quasi-mythical character, which the author repeats as he finds them recorded in Scripture, without committing himself to a statement that they are literally true, and leaving the reader to form his own opinion. Dionysius, after mentioning conflicting views on such incidents in early Roman history, often concludes with the phrase, slightly varied in the wording, "But let every one (of my hearers) judge as he will."[17] So Josephus ends his allusion to the longevity of the patriarchs with the words "But concerning these things let every one think as he pleases";[18] again, he has, he says, narrated the passage of the Red Sea as he found it described in the sacred books, and the credibility of the story is supported by a similar incident in the history of Alexander the Great, "but concerning these things let each decide as he thinks fit";[19] on the wonders of Sinai "let each of my readers think as he will, but I must narrate these things as they are recorded in the sacred books,"[20] and so constantly elsewhere.[21] In the century after Josephus this non-committal attitude on the marvellous has become an established doctrine for historians. Lucian

[14] Dionys., *Ant. Rom.* i. 64. 4. [15] *ib.* ii. 56. 2. [16] Or "haranguing" (ἐκκλησιάζοντα).

[17] Dionys., *Ant. Rom.* i. 48. 1 (κρινέτω δὲ ὡς ἕκαστος τῶν ἀκουόντων βούλεται), 48. 4 (ἐχέτω δ' ὅπῃ τις αὐτὸν πείθει), *cf.* ii. 40. 3, 70. 5, iii. 35. 5.

[18] *Ant. Jud.* i. 108. [19] *ib.* ii. 348. [20] *ib.* iii. 81.

[21] *ib.* iii. 268, 322, iv. 158, viii. 262, xix. 108: longer formulas in x. 281, xvii. 354 (with characteristic verbosity of this assistant): once in the *Jewish War* v. 257.

in his treatise on *How history should be written*[22] lays down the rule: " And should any myth come into question, it should be related but not wholly credited: rather it should be left open (ἐν μέσῳ θετέος) for readers to conjecture about it as they will, but do you take no risks and incline neither to one opinion nor to the other." Thus Josephus is here conforming to contemporary convention, but I have little doubt that Dionysius is again his immediate model.

From what has been said the author's motive is clear. He is embarking on a task never before attempted, though a beginning had been made at Alexandria, of presenting the complete history of his nation in the manner of contemporary pagan historians for the benefit of the world at large. This *magnum opus* must be cursorily dealt with in a lecture, and I can but touch on a few outstanding points. The work naturally falls into two nearly equal parts, the dividing-line being the close of the exile reached at the end of Book x. I may pass lightly over the earlier portion, based mainly on the Biblical record, because I shall have more to say on the author's text and interpretation of the Bible in my next lecture.

As a rule he closely follows the order of the Biblical narrative, but he has, with apologies to his countrymen,[23] rearranged and made a condensed and partial digest of the Mosaic code, reserving further treatment for a later work. Again, in the history of the Monarchy, he has naturally amalgamated the two accounts in *Kings* and *Chronicles*. He has been taxed, perhaps a little too severely, with " whitewashing" the history by omitting discreditable incidents. The omission of the story of the golden calf and the breaking of the first tables of the Law is the most glaring. On the other hand, unlike the Biblical Chronicler, he has not hesitated to tell the story of David's sin and the disastrous sequel.

[22] *Quomodo Hist. sit conscribenda* 60 (67).
[23] *Ant.* iv. 196 ff.

Besides the Bible, he quotes, wherever possible, external authority in support of it. Berosus the Babylonian, Manetho the Egyptian, Dius the Phoenician historian, Menander of Ephesus, the Sibylline oracles, the Tyrian records, Herodotus and others supply evidence on such matters as the flood, the longevity of the patriarchs, the tower of Babel, the correspondence of Solomon and Hiram, Sennacherib and Nebuchadnezzar. But his repertory here is limited, as is shown partly by his repetition of some of these passages in the *contra Apionem*, partly by the fact that more than once [24] a long array of names ends with that of Nicolas of Damascus, on whose Universal History he draws largely in his later books and who is probably here too his main authority. Some sources he knows only at second hand through Nicolas.

Occasionally the apologetic nature of the work shows itself in replies to those anti-Semite critics who are more fully confuted in the *contra Apionem*. The author would gladly omit the uncouth names of Jacob's descendants who accompanied him to Egypt, but feels bound to mention them in order to disprove the assertion of the Egyptian origin of his race.[25] Moses' laws on leprosy make the suggestion ridiculous that he himself was a leper.[26] The explanation of the three reasons why Moses did not take the direct route from Egypt to Palestine [27] is apparently another answer to current objections.

Personal animosity breaks out in one of those recurrent satirical attacks on the Samaritans,[28] " those versatile people who when they see the Jews prospering call them their kinsmen, claiming descent from Joseph and consequent relationship with them, but when they see them in danger assert that they have no connexion with them and are not bound to them by any tie of friendship or race, giving themselves out to be resident aliens." The story of King Saul is the occasion of two curious digressions, the first a reflection on the evil transformation of character produced by rise to power, the

---

[21] *Ant.* i. 94 f., 107 f.; *cf.* i. 159 f., vii. 101.   [25] *ib.* ii. 177.   [26] *ib.* iii. 265.
[27] *ib.* ii. 322 f.   [28] *ib.* ix. 291; *cf.* xi. 341, xii. 260.

second an encomium upon him as the type of the really brave man
who, knowing his predicted doom, unflinchingly goes out to battle
to meet it.[29]

In this connexion I may mention a strange encomium upon the
lawgiver, because the commendation of the particular merit for
which he is praised—his candour—has an indirect bearing on the
author's own practice with regard to the use of his sources, and
gives perhaps a rather sinister insight into his own mind. We are
told [30] that Moses "highly honoured" Balaam "by recording his
prophecies, and, though it was open to him to appropriate and take
the credit for them himself, as there would have been none to
convict him, he has given him this testimony and deigned to per-
petuate his memory." Similarly, in recording the advice of
Jethro to his son-in-law to delegate judicial duties to others, our
author extols the magnanimity of Moses in not concealing the fact
that this system did not originate with himself, "holding it right
to bear faithful testimony to merit, even though he might increase
his own reputation by taking credit for the inventions of others." [31]
This last passage, it is true, finds a partial parallel in Rabbinic
tradition; [32] but the two together illustrate the contemporary
practice of historians of absorbing and appropriating the work of
their predecessors without acknowledgment. Josephus did not
stand alone in regarding what we should call "plagiarism" as a
venial offence, and full acknowledgment of indebtedness as an
outstanding merit; but he affords a rather flagrant instance of
failure to imitate the lawgiver's candour.

Passing to the post-exilic history, which occupies the last ten
books of the *Antiquities*, we are given a patch-work, compiled
from such miscellaneous materials as were at the author's disposal.
The lack or abundance of available materials accounts for much
disproportion in the narrative; there are unfortunate gaps, notably

---

[29] *Ant.* vi. 262, 343 ff.   [30] *ib.* iv. 157 f.   [31] *ib.* iii. 73 f.
[32] *Sifre* (mentioned by J. Weill in Th. Reinach's French translation *in loc.*).

in the earlier portion, from the first return from exile down to the time of Antiochus Epiphanes, where a period of nearly four centuries is compressed into two books (xi–xii), while elsewhere the narrative expands into minute fulness, three whole books (indeed portions of four) being devoted to the reign of Herod the Great. For the story of the return and the period immediately following, for which we should welcome a second independent version to check and supplement the notoriously confused account in Ezra and Nehemiah, the author is solely dependent on the still less historical form of it contained in the Alexandrian Bible, the so called "Esdras A" and the Greek book of Esther. Some gleanings from the lives of Alexander the Great, the *Letter of Aristeas*, reproduced in a free paraphrase, and the story of Joseph the tax-collector, giving us a glimpse of the condition of Palestine under Ptolemaic rule, bridge the gulf down to the Maccabean age.

From the period of Antiochus Epiphanes down to the rise of Herod the Great the author has more abundant materials, and the main point of interest is the determination of the various sources— their number and value and the extent to which they are severally employed. The author plainly has used three main sources: the Greek first book of Maccabees, unnamed but freely paraphrased, and, when special Jewish documents begin to fail him, the two lost universal histories of pagan writers, Nicolas of Damascus and Strabo, who are constantly mentioned. Of these two Nicolas, who had served him occasionally from the opening of the *Antiquities* and continues to serve him down to the reign of Archelaus, is now his mainstay; Strabo is a subsidiary source. Polybius is twice mentioned;[33] beyond these authors it cannot be said with certainty that he has used others, except at second hand. But, having reached a period already partially covered in the *Jewish War*, he has, it seems, also had recourse to his earlier work, with a view to avoiding verbal repetition.

[33] *Ant.* xii. 135 f., 358 f.

In that earlier work his main source, as here, had been the invaluable Nicolas; but he has now accumulated a considerable mass of other materials, and in particular has discovered a first rate authority for the revolt under Antiochus Epiphanes and the rise of the Hasmonaean house, viz. the first book of Maccabees. Of that Alexandrian work the slighter sketch in the *War* shows no knowledge; and even now the author seems to have obtained only an imperfect copy of it. At any rate the parallels with that book stop short at the death of Jonathan,[34] and no use is made of the last three chapters which carry on the story up to the death of his brother Simon. It has been maintained that Josephus knew 1 Maccabees only in an earlier and shorter edition; I should rather be inclined to refer this omission to the imperfection of his MS. This book is the last of a corpus of Alexandrian versions of the later historical books of the Bible, from Samuel onwards, of which Josephus has fortunately obtained a copy, and the loss of the last few pages of a MS is a common phenomenon.

This whole question of investigation of sources, what the Germans call *Quellenkritik*, though a necessary and sometimes fascinating task for the historian, is apt perhaps to appear somewhat repellent. But there does arise at this point a problem of more general interest, affecting our author's method of work as a whole. A theory has been propounded, which raises the questions: Did Josephus make use of a large "anonymous" source, which embraced and had already combined into a larger whole those which he expressly names? Did he, whether through careless copying of his authorities or deliberately, lay claim to the work of others? Or did he himself, as he appears in places to assert, write a separate lost work on the history of Syria and adjacent countries?

It has been maintained by Destinon[35] that Josephus knew the 1st book of Maccabees and certain other documents only at second

---

[34] *Ant.* xiii. 212, 1 Macc. xiii. 30: the three following paragraphs in Josephus (213 ff.) possibly continue the dependence up to the end of 1 Macc. xiii.

[35] *Die Quellen des Fl. Josephus*, Kiel, 1882.

hand and that he appropriated, with but slight alterations, a work in which Jewish and pagan authorities had already been amalgamated. This theory is based upon the use of a little formula of reference, taking sometimes a personal, sometimes an impersonal form—"as we have shown" or "as has been shown elsewhere" (καθὼς ἐν ἄλλοις δεδηλώκαμεν or δεδήλωται). The phrase is constantly found in this portion of the *Antiquities* (Books xiii and xiv) at the close of paragraphs relating mainly to Syrian, sometimes to Parthian, history, where the writer breaks off and reverts to his main theme. In Book xiv the passive is always used, "as has been shown ἐν ἄλλοις," [36] or, in one instance,[37] "by others" (ὑπ' ἄλλων), where the reference to external authorities is unmistakable. But in the thirteenth book we consistently[38] find the personal phrase "as *we* have shown elsewhere," used in precisely the same way. In this book two sources have been amalgamated in alternate blocks, 1 Maccabees and another relating to Syrian history: a patch from Maccabees is followed by a patch from an unknown work, and the formula in question, referring the reader to some further source of information of Syrian history, occurs at the juncture, where the narrative of Maccabees is resumed. Destinon argues that the personal phrase must be read in the light of the impersonal expression found elsewhere, where the reference is undoubtedly to the work of others, and so far I should agree with him. But he further infers that the whole formula has been taken over unchanged from an older author, who wrote a separate work on Syria, and, since the formula only occurs at the points of juncture, as a sort of connecting-link between Syrian and Jewish history, he thinks that the amalgamation of these two elements in the narrative must have already been made in the anonymous source. Here I hesitate to follow him.

[36] *Ant.* xiv. 119, 270. [37] *ib.* xiv. 122.

[38] The personal form is attested in all the instances in this book (xiii. 36, 61, 108, 119, 186, 253 [cod. P], 271, 347, 371 f.), the impersonal form occasionally appearing as a variant reading in some MSS.

I believe, with Schürer, that this theory is unsound. It is on several grounds improbable. Though Josephus, like other historians, does not always mention his sources, it seems a needless complication to multiply their number, when so many are in fact either named or identifiable. He has elsewhere combined distinct sources himself, as in the case of Kings and Chronicles, and he may be given the credit of similar patchwork here. That he has made a *direct* use of 1 Maccabees is proved, to my mind, by the nature of the text. As will be shown in a later lecture, Josephus used a Greek Bible for the historical books from Samuel onwards containing a text of a peculiar type. This type of text persists in the extracts from Maccabees; and that the supposed anonymous writer should have likewise used just this particular recension of that book appears improbable. Moreover, the majority of our author's references are verifiable, and the formula which I have mentioned is not unlike others which he uses elsewhere: it is doubtless his own and not taken over from his source.

It remains to explain the use of the first person, the " we," which recalls a similar problem arising in the so-called " we passages " in the *Acts of the Apostles*. Careless as Josephus was and unscrupulous about taking personal credit for the work of others, I doubt whether he, any more than Luke, was so careless as repeatedly to take over such a phrase from his authority. Did he then write a separate work on Eastern history? We have no record of such activity, other than what may be inferred from a doubtful allusion of Jerome [39] to his having written on the seventy weeks of Daniel, a subject requiring a knowledge of Seleucid history. I think the true explanation probably lies in the direction suggested by Gutschmid and Drüner,[40] namely that Josephus refers to a preliminary work, perhaps a mere collection of excerpts, drawn up for his own use in connexion with the *Antiquities* and probably never published,

[39] Comm. on Isaiah, cap. 36, pref. to book xi, Vallarsi, vol. iv, p. 451 : see Drüner, *Untersuchungen über Josephus*, 1896, p. 78.

[40] *op. cit.* p. 80.

on Syria and Parthia. The tangled history of the later Seleucids would need such a *Vorarbeit,* and it is clear that he devoted considerable attention to Parthian affairs. Such a work might be indifferently referred to as his own or another's.

The reign of Herod the Great, which fills so large a space in our author's canvas, next calls for notice. That period of external splendour and internal oppression, with all the scandals of court intrigue and the horrors of the domestic tragedies, is vividly narrated on the basis of the record of a contemporary and intimate friend of the Idumaean monarch. Moreover, the story is told twice over: we have the briefer and more artistic account in the *Jewish War,* and the fuller picture covering three whole books in the *Antiquities.* The two accounts differ not merely in length, but in their arrangement and to some extent in their attitude to the principal figure. In the *War* the external history of prosperity, with the proud record of public buildings and benefactions, is kept distinct from the tragedies of the court: [41] in the *Antiquities* the events are told in chronological order. In the *War* the poignant narrative of the domestic dissensions leading up to the successive murders is told with all the pathos and the technical terminology of a Greek drama. We hear of Nemesis at the outset (i. 431), of the pollution of the house (638 μύσος, *cf.* 445), the tempest lowering over it (488), of the villain and "stage-manager of the whole abominable business" (530 τὸν λυμεῶνα τῆς οἰκίας καὶ δραματουργὸν ὅλου τοῦ μύσους), the anxious waiting of all Syria and Jewry for "the last act of the drama" (543) before sentence is finally passed on the unfortunate sons, the avenging deity (596 τὸν ἀλάστορα), the ghosts (δαίμονες) of the murdered sons roaming the palace and dragging secrets to light (599) or sealing the lips of others (607). The father appears throughout rather as the unfortunate victim of destiny, more sinned against than sinning. In the *Antiquities* this tragic element is wanting, and we have occasional outspoken condemnation of Herod.

[41] The break occurs at *B. J.* i. 431.

Thackeray.   5

The main source for both accounts, and the sole source for the
Jewish War, is undoubtedly the History of Nicolas of Damascus,
the close friend both of the Emperor Augustus and of Herod himself,
whom he championed and supported through thick and thin,
crowning his life of devotion to the father by assisting to secure
the succession to the throne of his son Archelaus. Nicolas, like
Herod, was son of an Antipater, a circumstance which may incidentally
have assisted to foster fraternal relations between the two. Besides
his historical works, Nicolas is reputed to have written tragedies,
and the dramatic presentment of the domestic tragedy in the *Jewish
War* and its severance from the external history might possibly
be attributed to him, rather than to Josephus or his colleagues.

In the *Antiquities* the subject receives much ampler treatment
and there are some discrepancies between the two narratives. The
assistant, who, as will be shown in a later lecture, here takes over
the work, has clearly received instructions from Josephus to avoid
repetition by thoroughly recasting the earlier account. To this end
he has apparently gone back to the original source, the History of
Nicolas, rearranged it in chronological order and made more extensive
use of it. But he has also access to other authorities. Allusion
is once made [42] to a distinct source—the " memoirs " or " commentaries " (ὑπομνήματα) of King Herod himself; but the form
of the sentence [43] suggests that he knew these only at second hand.
There are other reasons, however, for suspecting different and
perhaps conflicting sources, and in one instance we have what looks
like a duplication of a single story in different forms. Herod,
departing on a dangerous errand, leaves Mariamme in charge of
his uncle Joseph with instructions to kill her if he does not return: [44]
later on he assigns her to the keeping of Sohemus with similar
instructions: [45] both warders reveal their orders to the unfortunate
lady and pay the penalty with their lives. In the *War* the two

[42] *Ant.* xv. 174.

[43] i.e. the use of the imperfect tense περιείχετο, as Schürer points out.

[44] *Ant.* xv. 65.   [45] *ib.* xv. 202 ff.

incidents are merged into one. Among the sources other than Nicolas used in the *Antiquities* it is commonly held that there was one antagonistic to Herod. I must admit that I am not fully convinced that the occasional criticisms passed upon his character [46] may not come from Josephus himself; at any rate they are presented as his own.

Nicolas, the aristocratic friend of king and emperor, survived Herod and, in the rôle of king-maker, took an active part in the long and embittered controversy on the succession which ensued in Rome before Augustus. That scene,[47] with the embassies and counter-embassies, is narrated in great detail, including two speeches of Nicolas himself in support of Archelaus and his deceased friend. Nicolas is obviously still the reporter. And then this source, which has so long served Josephus in good stead, comes to an abrupt close. The historian is reduced to recounting anecdotes and dreams, and for the momentous period immediately following has but meagre materials.

Sixty years intervened between the deposition of Archelaus in 6 A.D., when Judaea was annexed to the Roman province of Syria, and the outbreak of war in 66. For the latter half of that period Josephus, born in the year of Caligula's accession (37), was alive; and it might be thought that the narrative was here largely based on his own recollections. In fact the contributions from that source appear to be slight; he is still dependent on documents both here and in the corresponding portion of the *Jewish War*. Dr. Eisler, in his forthcoming work on the Slavonic version of the *War*, shows how the events of this period there recorded largely turn on incidents of which an official record would be preserved in Rome: the historian has had recourse to state archives and *acta* immediately

[46] *ib.* xvi. 150 ff., 183 ff., 395 ff.

[47] Clearly forming the historical basis for the New Testament parable of the " nobleman " who went into a far country, " to receive for himself a kingdom," and of the embassy sent after him to say " We will not that this man reign over us," Luke xix. 12 ff.

at his door. The same seems to apply to the *Antiquities*, with
the difference that more use is there made of Roman literature
than of state papers.

In fact, for a large portion of the concluding books of the
Antiquities, the scene shifts from Palestine to Rome. The outstanding figure, forming the link between the two places, is again
a Herod, and the dramatic story of the rise of Agrippa I from
poverty, debt and imprisonment to his grandfather's throne is told
with some of the gusto and glamour of the earlier narrative of
Nicolas. Roman and Herodian history are in reality closely inter-
woven throughout this episode. Agrippa's varying fortunes are
associated with three successive emperors: imprisoned by Tiberius,
he is liberated and presented with a kingdom by his beloved Caligula,
and then, after his friend's assassination, on that proud day when
the tables are turned and a king of Judaea assists in the election
of a Roman emperor, he acts as mediator between senate and
army on the accession of Claudius. But this association, temporarily
so intimate, of king and emperor further serves as a peg on which
is hung much interesting, but strictly irrelevant, detail concerning
Roman court history. We have a digression on the dilatory policy
of Tiberius in the appointment of provincial governors, with the
reasons which he himself gave for it (including a little fable),[48] and
an allusion to his addiction to divination;[49] and here it is pertinent
to recall that at the very time when Josephus was writing this, the
gloomy emperor Domitian was studying the statecraft of his
predecessor. "Besides the commentaries and acts of Tiberius he
(Domitian) read nothing," says Suetonius,[50] and we can imagine that
he would not refuse Josephus access to this source and be com-
plimented by an allusion to his only literature. But the longest
digression of this sort is the extraordinarily full account of the
assassination of Caligula which fills the bulk of Book xix, with the

[48] *Ant.* xviii. 169–178.
[49] *ib.* 216.
[50] *Domit.* 20.

pictures of the growth of the conspiracy, the repeated delays, the final fixing of the day, the scene in the theatre, and the emperor's murder in the dark passage on his return from the games to the palace. All this is obviously drawn from a Latin source, and, since Mommsen, the writer has been commonly identified with M. Cluvius Rufus, a historian who figures once in Josephus' narrative [51] as quoting a line from Homer. Cluvius is known to have written the history of Nero, but whether his narrative went back to Caligula is uncertain. Any way Josephus has discovered a lively and circumstantial record, which, to eke out his scanty materials and make up the necessary tale of 20 books in imitation of his model, the Roman history of Dionysius,[52] he has not hesitated to incorporate entire, notwithstanding its irrelevancy to his proper subject. Throughout this portion, then, the sources appear to be a Roman history, possibly by Cluvius Rufus, a Herodian history [53] and some state documents.

Elsewhere too we find a preponderating Roman element. Thus the famous *testimonium Flavianum*, of which I shall have more to say in a later lecture, is preceded by the two incidents narrated of Pilate's governorship, which would be recorded in Roman *acta* in connexion with his later trial, and followed by two Roman scandals leading to the punishment of the priests of Isis and the banishment of all Jews from Rome.

From other—non-Roman—sources come two sketches of far Eastern Judaism: one relating to the Jews of Babylon and the brothers Asinaeus and Anilaeus, the freebooters who made themselves so formidable that their services were enlisted by the King of Parthia,[54] and the more pleasing story of the conversion to Judaism of the pious Helena, Queen of Adiabene and her son Izates,[55] also linked

[51] *Ant.* xix. 91 f.   [52] See above p. 56.

[53] Perhaps, as Hölscher suggests (*Die Quellen des Josephus*, p. 80), the main source, which has incorporated the Roman history.

[54] *Ant.* xviii. 310 ff.

[55] *ib.* xx. 17 ff.

up with Parthian history. Among the few items of purely Palestinian origin we have the list of high priests at the close of the whole work.

Of high value, if not quite so high as they are rated by one writer who calls them [56] " the most valuable documents which have come down to us from antiquity," are the state papers which Josephus inserts at various points in the latter half of the *Antiquities*.[57] These consist of decrees of the Roman senate, edicts of Julius Caesar, Mark Antony, Augustus, Agrippa, Claudius, and subordinate Roman officials, together with decrees of various communities of Asia Minor, usually in pursuance of orders received from Rome, granting and confirming to the Jews certain privileges to ensure the free exercise of their religion. Exemption from military service, protection of sabbath observance, freedom to hold religious meetings, to send without molestation money contributions to Jerusalem, and (in Asia) " to make prayer-houses beside the sea according to ancestral custom," prohibition of the stealing of their sacred books or money from the synagogue (σαββατεῖον), restoration of the charge of the sacred vestments to the high priests at Jerusalem—such are the topics of these documents. Their authenticity is now generally conceded. Josephus was not incapable of composing a correspondence between Hiram and Solomon or improvising speeches of Herod the Great and Agrippa: that was in accordance with contemporary convention. It was quite another matter to refer his readers, as he here does,[58] to the inscriptions engraved on brazen tablets still to be seen in the Capitol at Rome; here invention would lay him open to easy confutation. Whence did he obtain the documents? Suggestions that they had been previously collected by Nicolas of Damascus for his defence of the

[56] Gutschmid (quoted by Schürer).

[57] *Ant.* xiii. 260–264, xiv. 145–155, 190–264, 306–323, xvi. 162–173, xix. 280–291, xx. 11–14; in all 35 documents are quoted.

[58] *Ant.* xiv. 188, 266 (ἐναργῆ καὶ βλεπόμενα τεκμήρια παρεχόμεθα ... ἐπιδεικνύντες αὐτὰ χαλκαῖς στήλαις καὶ δέλτοις ἐν τῷ Καπετωλίῳ μέχρι νῦν διαμένοντα καὶ διαμενοῦντα).

Jews of Asia, or by King Agrippa II in connexion with the Alexandrian embassy of Philo, have nothing to recommend them. I have no doubt that Laqueur [59] is right in holding that they were collected by, or rather for, Josephus himself from the archives in Rome. Schürer [60] maintains that the Capitoline library could not have contained more than the Roman papers at most, certainly not the decrees of the cities of Asia Minor: these, he thinks, were collected from the various places. I doubt whether Josephus's own researches extended so far afield, and, as is urged by Willrich,[61] the Jewish provincial authorities would not be too ready to surrender copies of their papers to one whom they regarded as a traitor. But an injunction from imperial headquarters was a different thing and could not be disobeyed; and such a mandate had actually gone forth. We learn from Suetonius [62] that Vespasian restored the Roman Capitol, which with its library had been ruined in the conflicts of the year 69 " and undertook the restoration of 3,000 brazen tablets, which had at that time perished by fire, *copies from all quarters being investigated*: a most beautiful and ancient instrument of government," he continues, " in which are contained, almost from the foundation of the city, decrees of the senate, plebiscites concerning alliance and treaty and privilege granted to all and sundry." The orders to the provinces to send up copies of their state documents to Rome would probably not draw any hard and fast line, and the provincials would be likely to include all that were ultimately dependent on previous instructions received from Roman governors. Here then in Rome, whether in the Capitoline library or elsewhere, they were inspected and copied or rather, in most cases, translated, not by Josephus himself, who does not claim to have seen them, but by a colleague. If I am not mistaken, I can trace in these portions, the style of one of the author's able assistants, who has translated them, and the under-

[59] *Flavius Josephus* 227 f.
[60] *G. J. V.* (ed. 3) i. 86 note.
[61] *Urkundenfälschung*, 1924, p. 5.   [62] *Vesp.* 8 (quoted by Schürer).

lying Latin occasionally shines through.[63] The confused state of
the Greek text reveals in places the difficulty of the task.

I have now completed my brief and inadequate survey of the
historian's *magnum opus*. But before leaving it I should not omit
to touch on the concluding paragraphs—the peroration. The author
himself would doubtless expect his readers, however much they
might have "skipped" of the earlier narrative, to glance at this.
For the peroration, like the proem, was of a more personal character,
and in particular it was the place for advertisements: here the
reader might learn something of other forthcoming productions
from the same pen.

As was remarked in my first lecture, the *Antiquities* contains two
perorations, a longer and a shorter, written for distinct editions of
the work. They are not placed in chronological order. The longer
of them, written for the later edition, stands first. It begins "But
here I shall close my *Archaeology*, after which (he means "at the
point at which") I began my narrative of the war"; it includes a
brief *résumé* of the work, followed by some self-advertisement of
his exceptional qualifications, and ends with a statement that he
proposes to append a record of his life. This fixes the date as later
than 100 A.D., the year of King Agrippa's death, which is referred
to in the Autobiography.

Then follows the shorter and earlier peroration, which has been
retained in the later edition, though relegated to the end. Here we
find an allusion to further literary projects. The text runs (xx. 267 f.):
"But here I shall close the *Archaeology*, which is comprised in twenty
books and sixty thousand lines. And if the Deity permit, I shall
again give a summary description of the war and of what has
befallen us to this very day, which is in the thirteenth year of the
reign of the emperor Domitian, and the fifty-sixth of my own
life." But he has forgotten something and adds a further postscript.

---

[63] *e.g.* in the use of the dative (= Lat. ablative) absolute in place of the genitive,
Ant. xiv. 228 ff. Λευκίῳ Λέντλῳ Γαΐῳ Μαρκέλλῳ ὑπάτοις.

"I also propose to write (in) four books, in accordance with the opinions of us Jews, concerning God and His being, and concerning the laws, why under them some actions are permitted to us and others are forbidden."

Here there are one or two points of interest. We learn that the division into twenty books was the author's own, or rather, as I have said, was suggested to him by his unnamed model, the Roman *Archaeology* of Dionysius. The enumeration of lines or "stichometry," commonly appended as a separate note at the end of a MS, is here included in the text. The ordinary purpose of such enumeration was to fix the scriveners' pay: a statement is commonly appended at the end of the several books, and it has been established that scribes were paid by the hundred lines.[64] Here the round number is presumably approximate only and merely inserted to draw attention to the magnitude of the writer's task.[65] The date named is the year 93–4 A.D., some two years before the close of Domitian's reign and seven before the death of Agrippa: if it was taken in hand immediately after the completion of the Greek edition of the *War*, the larger work was some 18 years in the making.

But the main purpose of the paragraph is to advertise the two further projects. Neither of these, to our knowledge, ever saw the light, at least in the form here mentioned. We can infer from internal evidence that the *War*, like the *Antiquities*, passed through more than one edition; but of a summary sketch of the campaign, including the after history of the nation, there is no trace.

The other work, however, as we may infer from the mention of the four books and from scattered allusions in the *Antiquities* to its intended contents, had taken shape in the author's mind and already been begun. Two distinct topics are mentioned "Concerning God and His being" and "Concerning the laws, their sanctions and prohibitions, and the reasons for them."

[64] Rendel Harris, *Stichometry*, p. 26.

[65] In view of his habit of constantly reediting and introducing small changes into his work, it can hardly be intended as a safeguard against interpolations.

How much of the work was to be devoted to either topic
we cannot tell: possibly two separate works were contemplated.
Some part of the strictly theological portion has not improbably been
incorporated in the fine encomium on Judaism which closes the
contra Apionem. The other portion was to deal with "Customs
and causes," to use the short title by which he once [66] mentions it.
For this preparations had long since been made, indeed from the
time when the *Antiquities* was begun. Thus in the proem to that
work he writes: [67] "Those, however, who desire to examine the
reasons for everything (in the Mosaic law) will find food for much
philosophic reasoning, which I now defer, but on which, if God
grant me time, I shall endeavour to write after finishing the present
work." To this future treatise he relegates the fuller treatment of
various subjects mentioned in the *Antiquities*: the reason for circumcision,[68] the sacrifices (which were apparently to form a separate
section),[69] the shewbread,[70] the food-laws[71] and the Mosaic legis-
lation in general.[72] We may regret that the author did not live to
complete a work which might be expected to throw much light on
current Palestinian, and possibly Alexandrian, exegesis.

Here, without formal peroration, I will close my survey of the
Jewish Archaeology.

[66] *Ant.* iv. 198.   [67] *ib.* i. 25.   [68] *ib.* i. 192.
[69] *ib.* iii. 205 = 230 ἐν τοῖς περὶ θυσιῶν.
[70] *ib.* iii. 143, 257.   [71] *ib.* iii. 259.   [72] *ib.* iv. 198, 302.

JOSEPHUS AND JUDAISM:
HIS BIBLICAL TEXT

In previous lectures I have sketched the life of Josephus and briefly reviewed his two major works. It remains to attempt some estimate of the relation in which he stood to contemporary life and thought. The world in which he moved comprised three classes: his Jewish countrymen, the wider Greek-speaking community which he addressed (including his Roman patrons), and the little body of Christians just emerging from obscurity. I propose in this and subsequent lectures to offer some observations on the historian's relationship respectively to Judaism, to Hellenism and to Christianity. On the first and last of these heads I speak with diffidence. I am conscious that my present audience are far better qualified than I am to appraise our author's Hebraic affinities; while his relation to Christianity is, on more grounds than one, a highly controversial subject, the difficulty of which is increased by the fact that the latest evidence has not as yet been subjected to searching criticism, nor even been fully presented in an accessible form.

I am indeed aware of my temerity in attempting to criticize Josephus the Jew—to estimate the extent of his acquaintance with Rabbinical thought and the contributions of permanent importance to our knowledge of Judaism which we owe to this Hebrew of Jerusalem, priest and descendant of priests, proud of his connexion on his father's side with the first of the twenty-four priestly courses, on his mother's with the royal Hasmonaean house,[1] and, if we may

---

[1] Vita 1 f., cf. B.J. i. 3.

believe him, acknowledged by his compatriots to outstrip them all in the learning of his race.[2] This last proud boast is, indeed, immediately followed by a modest admission that he never succeeded in mastering the pronunciation of Greek; and here I am happy to follow his example, knowing that I lay myself open to the charge of a defective grounding, not only in Hebrew pronunciation, but in Rabbinical lore.

Yet, it must, I think, be granted, that these high pretensions lead us to expect something more than we receive: the author's contribution to our knowledge not only of the deeper religious aspects of Judaism, but even of its ritual, customs and antiquities, is somewhat disappointing. We are conscious of a certain superficiality, partly attributable, no doubt, to the Greek audience which he addresses, but largely also to character and training. He excels as a popularizer of the external history of his nation and, in his latest work, as an apologist. But as profound theologian and religious devotee he is wanting, or at least rarely betrays such deeper knowledge and emotions in his works. He lacks the erudition and piety of the Palestinian Rabbi, the rapt mysticism of the Alexandrian Philo. As has recently been said by Professor Moore, " it may be fairly inferred that Josephus, like most of the aristocratic priesthood to which he belonged, had little interest in religion for its own sake, and that his natural antipathy to all excess of zeal was deepened by the catastrophe which religious fanatics had brought upon his people." [3] His fine apology for Judaism, the contra Apionem, must not, however, be forgotten, where he does rise to a higher level and display a sincere and impassioned zeal for his country's religion. Apart from that noble legacy, probably the most important contributions which we owe to him are the information which he indirectly supplies on the Biblical texts current in the first century, and, to a less degree, a miscellaneous mass of traditional lore or Haggadah. I propose to concentrate on the author's Bible and his Biblical traditions; but, before I pass to those

[2] Ant. xx. 263.   [3] G. F. Moore, Judaism i. 210.

matters, a few words must be said on the subject of language and some strange explanations which he incidentally gives of some Hebrew proper names.

The "language of his forefathers"[4] in which Josephus composed the first draft of his *Jewish War* was doubtless Aramaic, of which he must have had a thorough mastery. Was his knowledge of Hebrew equally profound? It seems impertinent to question the proficiency of the learned priest in the language of Scripture. Yet others more competent to express an opinion have concluded that his knowledge was "superficial."[5] The test to which he lays himself open is his translation of proper names. Many of these are correct enough according to the standards of his time; some were taken over from his Bible, whether Hebrew or Greek. But others are, to say the least, slipshod or actually inaccurate. It is true, as Professor Moore reminds us,[6] that such "interpretations of names were not put forth for the satisfaction of modern philologists but for the edification of ... contemporaries," and must not be over-stressed. The Professor is speaking of etymologies, even worse, perpetrated by the Alexandrian Philo. Josephus knew better than to suggest, as Philo does, *Greek* derivations for Semitic words, *e. g.* to connect *Pascha* with the verb πάσχειν "to suffer" or "Euphrates" with εὐφραίνειν.[7] Still we have a right to expect from the Palestinian priest greater exactitude than in the following instances. Eve (Εὕα), he says,[8] signifies (σημαίνει) "mother of all"; his Bible (Gen. iii. 20) told him that Adam called his wife *Hawwah* ("Living" or "Life") "because she was the mother of all"; but that is not what Josephus states. However, this may be attributed rather to indolence than to ignorance: "that is good enough for my Greek readers." On the year of Jubilee he states[9] that the word ἰάβηλος signifies "freedom"; this he takes from the LXX rendering "year

---

[4] *B.J.* i. 3 τῇ πατρίῳ (γλώσσῃ).

[5] Edersheim, art. *Dict. of Christian Biography* iii. 452 b, quoting Ewald's judgment "weak in his Hebrew."

[6] *Judaism* i. 322.   [7] Siegfried, *Philo von Alexandria* 196.   [8] *Ant.* i. 36.   [9] *ib.* iii. 283.

of release" (ἐνιαυτὸς ἀφέσεως), ignoring the traditional Hebrew
meaning "ram" or "ram's horn." With this may be linked his
explanation of Gilgal or Galgala, "this word means 'free'"; [10] the
only freedom discoverable here is the liberty taken by the author in
this loose paraphrase of the correct Biblical explanation, the *rolling
away* of the reproach of Egypt.[11] The interpretation of Samson,
"the name means strong" [12] is probably guesswork, the connexion
with *Shemesh* "Sun" being practically certain. Philology clearly
cannot be regarded as the historian's *forte*. Yet, as already said,
these instances must not be overemphasized, and it is perhaps
precarious to draw inferences from them as to his comparative
knowledge of the two Semitic languages, since this looseness of
interpretation extends even to Aramaic forms. With reference to
Pentecost, the Hebrew *'atzereth*, he writes [13] "the feast which the
Hebrews call ἀσαρθά means fiftieth'"; had he said "is called
Pentecost by the Greeks," he would have been correct, but no
etymology of the Semitic word can, I imagine, support this alleged
numerical sense.[14] In one curious instance, the name of Reuben,
he deserts the Hebrew text and significantly adopts the Syriac and
possibly older form, writing Ῥουβῆλος (Syr. *Rubil*), which he inter-
prets as "by the mercy of God." [15] How he extracted the meaning
"mercy" out of the first syllable is uncertain; but this agreement
with the Syriac, and the use of Aramaic forms like ἀσαρθά and
others,[16] suggest that he was perhaps more conversant with Aramaic
than with Hebrew, and, when not using a Greek Bible, would turn
more naturally to a Targum than to the original text.

[10] Or "liberal" (ἐλευθέριον), *ib*. v. 34.   [11] Joshua v. 9.   [12] *Ant*. v. 285.   [13] *ib*. iii. 252.

[14] Similarly in *B. J.* v. 151 he speaks of Beth-zaith (= "house of olives"), the northern
suburb of Jerusalem, as "the recently built quarter called in the vernacular Bezetha,
which might be translated into Greek as New Town"; but ii. 530 "the district called
Bezetha *and also* New Town" (τὴν καὶ Καινόπολιν) shows that he knew better.

[15] *Ant*. i. 304 (κατ' ἔλεον τοῦ θεοῦ); see *Encycl. Bibl.* iv. col. 4091.

[16] *e. g.* for articles of the high priest's vestments; in *Ant*. iii. 156 he knows both the
Heb. *abnet* and the Aramaic (*h*)*emian*, introduced by "the Babylonians." He substitutes
the Aramaic Diglath for the Heb. Ḥiddeḳel, but translates the latter, *ib*. i. 39.

Passing to another subject, we find a similar departure from normal Rabbinical practice in a well-known passage in the *contra Apionem*,[17] on the *canon* of Scripture, where Josephus contrasts the 22 " accredited " books of his race with the " myriads of inconsistent and conflicting books " of other nations. I must not linger on the notorious difficulties of this passage. Josephus implies that the canon had long been closed; whereas we know that almost at the time when he was writing the canonicity of two books, Song of Songs and Ecclesiastes, was being debated by Palestinian Rabbis. Again, though he gives a tripartite arrangement of Scripture, it is not the normal division—Law, Prophets, Writings; four books only remain in his third category,[18] the historical books outside the Pentateuch being all placed in the second; and the total number is not the normal 24, but 22. We cannot adopt the view suggested by Grätz that Josephus rejected the two disputed books; for we find this same total of 22 in lists, which enumerate the several books and are given by Christian writers (Origen and Jerome) who were in touch with and derived their information from Palestinian tradition, and who moreover associate the number 22 with the number of letters in the Hebrew alphabet. The constituent books intended, but not named, by Josephus were doubtless the same as those enumerated by these writers, the total being reduced from 24 to 22 by uniting Ruth with Judges and Lamentations with Jeremiah. When we find Origen [19] giving a list which includes the Hebrew titles and states " Judges, Ruth, with them (i. e. with the Hebrews) in one," " Jeremiah with Lamentations and the Epistle in one," we are led to infer that this strange division of the Bible attested by Josephus was not peculiar to himself or to the Alexandrian school but had support in some Palestinian circles.

[17] *c. Ap.* i. 37 ff.   [18] viz. those " containing hymns to God [= Psalms + Song of Songs] and precepts for the conduct of human life [= Proverbs + Ecclesiastes]."

[19] *ap.* Eusebius *Hist. Eccl.* vi. 25; *cf.* iv. 26 (for Melito's eastern researches) and Jerome's Preface to Samuel and Kings (showing acquaintance with three reckonings—22, 24 and 27 books). Dr. C. J. Ball has shown that " the Epistle of Jeremy " is not an original Greek composition but a free paraphrase of a lost Hebrew text.

I pass on to consider the *Biblical text* of Josephus, a matter which, in view of the historian's date, is of considerable importance. First century witnesses to the letter of Scripture are few: indeed we can name only one earlier writer who quotes it freely, viz. Philo, and Philo's quotations are practically confined to the Pentateuch. In the large use which he makes of the later historical books Josephus stands alone, and his evidence antedates our earliest complete MS in any language, the Greek Codex Vaticanus, by nearly three centuries—a period during which the text did not remain unaltered. Widening divergence between local varieties of text led to various revisions on the part of both Jewish and Christian scholars, with a view to establishing the *Hebraica veritas* and checking the progress of corruption. A witness who takes us far back behind the three local recensions of the Greek Bible known to Jerome in the 4th century, behind the Hexapla of Origen in the 3rd, and even behind or at least to the opening days of the great Rabbinical school of Jamnia at the end of the first, carries therefore considerable weight.

What was the nature of the text, or texts, which Josephus employed? Whence did they emanate and what is their precise worth? What part did he himself take in the task of translation, and how much does he owe to the labours of predecessors? Those are some of the questions which arise, and the results which seem to emerge are not without interest and importance.

The historian himself would lead us to suppose that he translated the Hebrew Scriptures himself. "This work which I have undertaken," he writes in the proem to the *Antiquities*,[20] "... will contain the complete account of our ancient history and constitution translated (μεθηρμηνευμένην) from the Hebrew Scriptures"; elsewhere [21] he states, less equivocally, "At the outset of my work... I remarked that I was merely translating (or "paraphrasing," μεταφράζειν) the books of the Hebrews into the Greek language and promised to repeat the story without omission or addition on my own part." [22]

---

[20] *Ant.* i. 5.　　　[21] *ib.* x. 218.　　　[22] *Cf.* also *Ap.* i. 1.

These statements, like others of their author, are not to be taken at their face value without reservations. The broad result revealed by a careful study of his use of Scripture is that he employed at least two texts, one in a Semitic language, the other in Greek. Sometimes one was used almost to the exclusion of the other: sometimes both were consulted and amalgamated. I speak of a Semitic language, because the adjective which he uses, Ἑβραϊκός, might, like the adverb Ἑβραϊστί in the N. T., include Aramaic, and, while it is probable that he has sometimes gone back to the original Hebrew, there are also indications in places that he is dependent on a Targum. As regards the respective use made of his two Bibles, a clear line of demarcation can be drawn at the close of the Octateuch: perhaps I should rather say at the close of the Pentateuch, for his text of the three books which immediately follow it in the Greek Bible (Joshua, Judges, Ruth) stands a little apart. Throughout the Pentateuch his main authority is a Semitic text, and the use made of the so-called " Septuagint " is slight; here he is presumably justified in claiming that the translation is his own. From Samuel onwards to the end of the historical books the position is reversed: the basis of his text is a Greek Bible, and the Semitic text is only a subsidiary source. Here he found a large part of his work already done for him, his own share being confined to polishing the style and removing what he considered the vulgarisms of the existing translation. For the three intervening books (Joshua, Judges, Ruth) I find no certain evidence for the use of a Greek text; as between Hebrew and Aramaic, I suspect, in Judges at least, dependence on a Targum.

I do not propose to dwell on the historian's Hebrew or Aramaic Bible, but to concentrate on what to me is the more interesting subject—the nature of the Greek text which lay before him. Two instances may, however, first be quoted to show the apparent influence of a Targum. My illustrations throughout will be drawn from the Books of Samuel and Kings, in which, though he is mainly dependent on his Greek Bible, he occasionally has recourse to a

Semitic text. In the first Book of Kings [23] we are told that the
repentant Ahab "fasted and lay in sackcloth and went *softly*." The
word translated "softly" is the substantive אט "quietness," here
used adverbially; the Greek MSS either omit it or render "bent"
or "bowed down" (κεκλιμένος). The Targum, however, has
יָחֵף "barefoot," and that was also the text found in his source by
Josephus who writes γυμνοῖς τοῖς ποσὶ διῆγεν.[24] In another instance
it is the Targum, again with Josephus as its sole companion, which
introduces the idea of "quietly," where all other texts have the
reverse. The driving of Jehu was, according to these texts, unmistakable to distant spectators by its furiousness;[25] but the Tar-
gumist in place of "madly" has "quietly"[26] and Josephus follows
him, writing "for he was advancing leisurely and in good order."[27]
The author of this text, to whom the quiet driver was a remarkable
phenomenon, might almost be thought to have suffered from the
pace of the modern motorist! One further instance of dependence
on a Semitic text will suffice: the witch consulted by Saul dwelt,
according to Josephus, not at Endor, but "in the city of Dor."[28]
Here there has been confusion between final *Nun* and *Resh* and עין
has been read as עיר.

But, as I said, it is the Greek Bible of Josephus which is of
main interest. Dependence on the Greek is obvious in the use
made of whole books, Alexandrian paraphrases of Scripture, such
as the so called 1st Esdras, including the fable, of purely Greek
origin, of the three pages of Darius, the Greek Esther with similar
interpolations, or the 1st book of Maccabees, drawn from the
extant Greek and not from the lost Hebrew original. It is evident
again in the acquaintance shown with isolated Greek glosses in
the earlier books, as when Josephus takes over from the LXX that

---

[23] 1 K. xxi. 27 (= LXX 3 Regn. xx. 27).

[24] *Ant.* viii. 362; *cf.* vii. 202 where he translates יחף in precisely the same way.

[25] 2 K. ix. 20 (בשגעון, LXX ἐν παραλλαγῇ).

[26] בנייח.

[27] *Ant.* ix. 117.

[28] *Ant.* vi. 330, 1 Sam. xxviii. 7.

vapid reply of David to Goliath's question " Am I a dog? "—" No but even worse than a dog." [29]

Not only, however, can we confidently state in general terms that Josephus used *a* Greek Bible. We can go further and identify the particular type of Greek text which lay before him. This text was not one of those contained in our oldest uncial MSS, the codex Vaticanus or Alexandrinus, on which our modern printed editions of the Septuagint are based. It was a text allied to one preserved only in a small group of MSS, written not in uncial but in cursive script at a much later date, between the 10th and the 14th centuries, and known by the figures assigned to them by the eighteenth century editors, Holmes and Parsons, as 19, 82, 93 and 108. This type of text, which has survived only in these late and, as might be thought, insignificant MSS, was in the nineteenth century identified with a particular recension of the Greek Bible current in Syria and adjacent countries in the fourth century and commonly designated "Lucianic" after its supposed author, the Christian Lucian of Antioch, who suffered martyrdom under the emperor Maximin in the year 311 or 312. And now that we have in our hands fuller and more accurate editions both of the Septuagint and of Josephus, we discover that this "Syrian" text in an older form was in existence more than two centuries earlier, and can be carried back from the age of the Christian Lucian to that of the Jewish historian.

This marked "Lucianic" character of Josephus' Biblical text is a fact of considerable importance in the earlier history of the Greek Bible; and to show its significance I will venture to digress for a little and briefly recall the principal stages in that history. The Greek Bible, being a translation of a Hebrew text older by a millennium than the earliest dated Hebrew MS, claims our respect at least on the ground of antiquity; and for all its imperfections, it does constantly provide the materials for the reconstruction of an older Hebrew, superior to that contained in our modern Bibles.

[29] *Ant.* vi. 186, 1 Regn. (1 Sam.) xvii. 43.

It was the production of Alexandrian scholars during the last two and a half centuries before our era. The *Letter of Aristeas,* giving the traditional story of its origin, however fabulous some of its details may be, is at least correct in confining the original undertaking to the Pentateuch and dating it in the early Ptolemaic era. Josephus is perfectly correct in limiting the work of these pioneers, the " Seventy " so called, to the *Torah*; he does not, like later writers, represent them as translating the whole Bible, and possibly he did not associate with Alexandria at all the versions of the later historical books, which he has used so freely in a recension current in Syria. These versions of the later books followed in the next century or two, first the Prophets, probably, like the *Torah,* an fficial production, and then the " Writings," treated with greater freedom as national literature, but not yet canonical. By the beginning of our era the work was practically complete and widely current, even in Palestine. But this old Greek Bible now passed into other hands. Two causes, animosity against the first converts to Christianity who had appropriated and, as was alleged, distorted the LXX for their own ends, together with a just sense of the laxity and inadequacy of some of the Alexandrian versions, produced a revulsion of feeling and a final abandonment of the work by the Palestinian leaders. The Dispersion, however, still needed a Greek Bible, and the demand for stricter accuracy and adherence to the current Hebrew led in the second century to a large output of new translations in Asia Minor based on the text of R. Akiba and his school. We possess fragments of the work of three of these translators, Aquila of Pontus, Theodotion of Ephesus, and Symmachus, possibly of Cappadocia. In the third century the outstanding event is the production of Origen's great work, the *Hexapla,* designed to bring the LXX into line with the current Hebrew by the aid of the Asiatic translations, which with the other texts were set out in parallel columns. Origen's attempt to produce a standard Greek text was unsuccessful, and different localities continued to use their rival recensions. In the fourth century, as we learn from a well-known passage of Jerome, three such recensions held the field: "Alexandria and Egypt acclaim Hesychius as their authority: the region from Constantinople to Antioch approves the copies of Lucian the martyr: the intermediate Palestinian provinces read the MSS which were promulgated by Eusebius and Pamphilus on the basis of Origen's labours, and the whole world is divided between these three varieties of text." [30]

Now the endeavour of the modern editor of the Septuagint is to recover the oldest form of the text, and for this purpose he has to work backwards from the date of our oldest extant MS, the fourth century codex Vaticanus. His first task is to detect and segregate the three fourth century recensions mentioned by Jerome—Hesychian, Lucianic and Eusebian. The Lucianic text has in large measure been identified through an ancient note stating that its readings were marked by the letter *Lamed* and the discovery of this mark in certain passages in a Paris MS: the Eusebian text is also known. The next stage is to get back behind the *Hexapla* of Origen, which was largely the cause of subsequent mixture of texts. And here comes in the importance of the evidence of Josephus in showing us that one form of text, the Lucianic, has survived, with minor alterations, from a period not only earlier than Lucian, but a century and a half earlier than Origen.

Lucian's Antiochene text, current throughout Northern Syria and Asia Minor in the fourth century, is based on an older text current, apparently in the same region, before the end of the first. Josephus is not the only person who has built on and been given the credit for other men's labours; we are forced to postulate an *ur-Lucian*. Before Origen's time the Greek Bible apparently existed in two main types of text, a pre-Lucianic or Syrian form used by Josephus on the one hand, and an Alexandrian on the other.

The Josephan Biblical text is *uniformly* of this Lucianic type from 1 Samuel to 1 Maccabees. He has, for this large portion of Scripture, used a single Bible, not two or more; and, were it not

[30] *Praef. in Paralipp.*

that in his day the codex form of book was hardly in existence, and that the papyrus scrolls are believed to have been small and confined to not more than a book or two, I should be tempted to think that he has used a single MS, mutilated at the beginning and end. Take the last historical book which he uses, 1 Maccabees. Here, in the first place, the persistence of the "Lucianic" type of text militates, as I said, against the theory that he knows the book only at second hand through some anonymous writer who has already incorporated the bulk of it; it is improbable that his predecessor should here have employed precisely the same recension as Josephus uses throughout. Again, he shows no knowledge of the last three chapters of that book. Here it is maintained that he knew the work in a shorter edition. I should rather suggest that his MS was defective at the close; and it is perhaps significant that there is a similar indication of loss of leaves at the beginning. In 1 Samuel the "Lucianic" element does not make its appearance for the first six or seven chapters.[31]

Where did the historian obtain his Greek Bible? He shows no acquaintance with it in that short sketch of Maccabaean history in the *Jewish War*, and this ignorance of it in his earlier work, together with the fact that the old Latin version of the Greek Bible, the *Vetus Itala*, has affinities with the "Lucianic" text, might suggest that his Greek Bible was not among the books which he brought with him from Palestine,[32] but was found in Rome. However this may be, I have no doubt that its ultimate place of origin was northern Syria. Next to "Lucian," the Biblical text most nearly allied to the historian's is that of Symmachus,[33] and Symmachus was an Asiatic; the only recorded incident in his life is placed in Cappadocia. The text of Lucian in the fourth century was current

---

[31] The first clear instance is in 1 Regn. viii. 8, ἔργα and ἐξήγαγ (ον) *vice* ποιήματα and ἀνήγαγον (*Ant.* vi. 38). Still he has Greek "additions" in 1. R. i. 21 (*Ant.* v. 346, mention of tithes) and v. 6, vi. 1 (*Ant.* vi. 3, the plague of mice).

[32] *Cf. Vita* 418 βιβλίων ἱερῶν.

[33] In 1 Regn. we have parallels with Symmachus in xiii. 20 (ὕνιν), xv. 23 (ἀπειθεῖν), 30 (τιμῆσαι), xvi. 21 (ὁπλοφόρος), *cf.* xxxi. 4, xvii. 39 (+ ἀγύμναστος γάρ εἰμι).

from Constantinople to Antioch, i.e. throughout Asia Minor and N. Syria; and it is probable that the parent text used by Josephus had much the same range. We can hardly suppose that this Greek version was wholly indigenous to Syria; but who was the real author of this Antiochene recension of the Alexandrian Bible, and how much older it may be than Josephus, we do not know.

A few instances of "Lucianic" readings of Josephus must suffice. I draw my examples again from the books of Samuel. In 2 Sam. xxiii. 11, in the narrative of the exploits of David's mighty men, we read in the Masoretic text that "the Philistines were gathered together לַחַיָּה," which yields no tolerable sense. The English and American revised versions render "into a troop," as from חַיָּה "a clan." The majority of the Greek MSS seem correctly to recognise that the word is a place-name, rendering εἰς Θηρία (לַחַיּוֹת); but we cannot identify any place bearing the strange name of "Wild beasts." The correct name appears only in Josephus (Ant. vii. 310), in the MSS representing the "Lucianic" text and in the Armenian version, which have "to (a place called) Jawbone"; we recognise at once Lehi, a name which the Philistines had good cause to remember as the scene of a famous exploit of Samson.[34] In the next chapter, 2 Sam. xxiv. 22, the various Greek renderings of an agricultural instrument seem to preserve local distinctions, suggestive of their place of origin. Araunah the Jebusite offers David the oxen at work on the threshing-floor for a burnt offering and the threshing-instruments (Heb. הַמֹּרִגִּים) for fuel. For "threshing-instruments" most Greek MSS have "the wheels" (οἱ τρόχοι), meaning the threshing-*waggon* on rollers "not used in Palestine... rare in Syria (except in the north) but ... the usual instrument in Egypt."[35] Here evidently we have the Alexandrian rendering. The Lucianic text, as often, has two words for one, "the boards and the ploughs" (τὰ ξύλα καὶ τὰ ἄροτρα); Josephus (Ant. vii. 331) has "the ploughs" alone. The "boards" doubtless mean the threshing-

[34] Jd. xv. 9 ff.

[35] Driver, *Joel and Amos* (*Camb. Bible*, 1915), p. 232 f.; *Encycl. Bibl.* i. 82 f.

board or drag usual in Syria and Palestine; [36] the "ploughs" possibly indicate Arabic influence, מוֹרַג being a loan-word in Arabic, with the meaning "ploughshare." [37] Here the Biblical text of Josephus is in partial agreement with Lucian, and, whether emanating from Syria or from Arabia in the larger sense, clearly does not come from Egypt.

Another curious case of approximation of the Josephan and Lucianic texts occurs in 1 Sam. xxiii. 25, where we read in the M. T. of David's taking refuge from Saul "in the wilderness of Ma'on." The geography in this context shows that Ma'on is right; but both in Josephus and in Lucian an intrusive initial *shin* has converted the proper name into *Shim'on*. The two texts differ, however, in one respect: Josephus (*Ant.* vi. 280) retains the Semitic name unaltered, "in the wilderness of Simon;" Lucian translates it by ἐπήκοος, "into the listening wilderness," as in fact Josephus does elsewhere. [38] As is suggested by Mez, [39] the exemplar of Josephus is probably not Semitic, but an earlier form of the Lucianic text which left *Shim'on* untranslated. The intrusive letter was presumably the abbreviated relative pronoun, used, like ד in the Targum on this passage, as a mark of the genitive.

A final minor coincidence may be mentioned. Josephus, in common with Lucian, places David's death at the close of a book. A natural arrangement, indeed, but it is not that adopted either by the Masoretes or by the bulk of the Greek MSS, which attach David's old age to the reign of his successor narrated in the first book of

---

[36] *Ibid.*   [37] Hebrew Lexicon, Brown-Driver-Briggs *s. v.*

[38] *Ant.* i. 304 " The name Σεμεών signifies that God listened (ἐπήκοον γεγονέναι) to her." Rahlf's suggestion, *Septuaginta-Studien*, Heft 3, 87, that " ἐπηκόῳ ist = שמע, denn ἐπακούειν gibt öfter ענה als שמע wieder," is therefore highly improbable.

[39] *Die Bibel des Josephus*, Basel, 1895, p. 29 f. Another curious case of approximation of the Josephan and a Syrian text, both being ultimately dependent upon a Targum, is noted by Mez, p. 32. In 1 Sam. xxviii. 1, for M.T. לצבא " for warfare," Josephus (*Ant.* vi. 325) has εἰς 'Ρεγ(γ)άν, an apparent corruption for εἰς Φάραγγα(ν), " into the valley," which actually stands in the Peshitto (לנחלא). The confusion, as Mez points out, is only intelligible through the medium of an Aramaic Targum, in which חילא = both הצבא (warfare) and גיא (valley).

Kings. I believe that curious arrangement to be attributable to an attempt to make Samuel and Kings into volumes of more equal dimensions, and that the more natural division of books in Lucian and Josephus is also the older.[40]

So much for our author's text of the historical books. Of the prophetical books naturally little use is made, apart from the narrative chapters of Jeremiah, and, if we may include it under this category, as Josephus would have done, the Book of Daniel. He appears to have used a Greek Daniel combining the peculiarities of the two known versions; in Jeremiah [41] and in the slight allusions to the other *Nebiim* I find no certain evidence of acquaintance with a Greek text. We have a strange allusion [41a] to predictions of the calamities of Jerusalem, including its capture by the Romans, attributed to Jeremiah and Ezekiel, the latter of whom is said to have written *two* books on the subject; but the text is doubtful and the last clause may originally have referred to two books of Jeremiah, viz. the prophecy and the Lamentations. The only definite prediction of Isaiah mentioned is quoted at second hand, namely the prophecy of the erection of an altar to the Lord in the land of Egypt,[42] on which Onias relied in building the schismatic temple at Leontopolis.[43] The story of Jonah is told somewhat apologetically " as I found it recorded ";[44] and we are given a paraphrase of Nahum's prediction of the fall of Nineveh, the only prophetical passage showing possible dependence on a Greek text.[44a]

---

[40] I may refer to my Schweich Lectures, *The Septuagint and Jewish Worship*, p. 19.

[41] In *Ant.* x. 175 (εἴς τινα τόπον Μάνδρα λεγόμενον) Josephus preserves a better text of Jer. xli (xlviii) 17 than the M.T. which has " to the lodging (גרות, ? khan) of Chimham." Μάνδρα (= גדרות, Zeph. ii. 6 LXX) is the " fold " or " enclosure," and its position " by Bethlehem " is suggestive, in view of the N.T. story of the shepherds (Luke ii. 8). Aquila (ἐν τοῖς φραγμοῖς) had the same text.   [41a] *Ant.* x. 79.

[42] Is. xix. 19.

[43] *B.J.* vii. 432, *Ant.* xiii. 64. A general allusion is made to the " books " left by Isaiah and to the δωδεκαπρόφητον in *Ant.* x. 35.

[44] *Ant.* ix. 208 ff.   [44a] *ib.* 239-241.

Apart from Law and Prophets, using the latter term in the wider sense to include the historical books, I should be inclined to assign a separate place to certain " writings deposited in the temple " which Josephus expressly mentions on three occasions, and to which he possibly alludes more vaguely elsewhere. As these passages, with one doubtful exception, all refer to lyrical portions of Scripture, I venture to regard them as references, not to the sacred scrolls of the Law and the Prophets, but to a separate collection of chants, taken mainly from the Bible, for the use of the temple singers. The first, which is the doubtful instance, runs: [45] " A writing deposited in the temple shows that God predicted to Moses that water would thus spring from the rock." Here I think the reference is to the little song to the well in Numbers,[46] with the preceding promise to Moses of a miraculous gift of water: " From thence to Beer—that is the well whereof the Lord said unto Moses, Gather the people together and I will give them water." And then, rather inconsequently, because it refers to water produced by human exertion, follows the song, once probably included in the old book of Jashar, " Then sang Israel this song, Spring up O well," and so on. If my suggestion here is not wholly erroneous, the temple hymn-book must have included beside the song the prefatory prediction. Again, we are told of Moses' song [47] that [48] " he read them a poem in hexameter verse, which he has also left in a book in the temple,[49] containing a prediction of things to come "; and again, of Joshua,[50] " that the length of the day was then increased and surpassed its usual measure is attested by writings deposited in the temple." Here we have an allusion to Joshua's incantation to the sun, which in the extant text includes a statement of its fulfilment, and which, as we are there told, stood in the old national song-book known as the book of Jashar. To these three passages I should be inclined to add two

---

[45] *Ant.* iii. 38.   [46] Numb. xxi. 16 ff.   [47] Deut. xxxii; *cf.* xxxi. 19 ff.   [48] *Ant.* iv. 303.
[49] ἐν βίβλῳ ἐν τῷ ἱερῷ: Weill (in the French translation edited by Th. Reinach) erroneously renders " dans le livre saint."
[50] *Ant.* v. 61 (Joshua x. 12 f.).

others relating to dirges, one extant and one lost, which, though the temple is unnamed, are here stated to have been preserved until the writer's time. " (David) wrote also lamentations and funeral eulogies on Saul and Jonathan, which have survived to my day," [51] and, we may add, were also included in the book of Jashar; [52] elsewhere [53] we read that " Jeremiah the prophet composed a funeral elegy on (Josiah) which survives even until now." This last may be drawn from a similar statement in Chronicles,[54] but should rather, I think, be ranked with the other passages as resting on personal knowledge. Lastly the statement that Moses' song at the Red Sea [55] was composed " in hexameter rhythm " [56] connects it with his other song in Deuteronomy and suggests possible adaptation for a temple choir.

Josephus more than once asserts that he has added nothing, or nothing of his own, to the Biblical narrative.[57] We need not scrutinize his meaning too closely, or ask whether, as a Pharisee, he regarded the rich store of tradition which he has incorporated as part and parcel of Scripture. Anyhow, he has, to attract his Greek readers, diversified the record with a mass of legendary matter, which is of considerable interest to us. He has culled from all quarters: Alexandria and even the *Sibylline Oracles* have contributed their quota. But a large proportion find parallels, or partial parallels, in the Rabbinic works, which were not compiled until a century or more later, and these, with other traditions for which no parallel can be traced, may be regarded as a valuable collection of first century *Midrash*. Here it is but possible to touch on a large theme, which has been fully, I do not know whether exhaustively, dealt with by Rabbinic scholars.[58]

---

[51] *Ant.* vii. 6.   [52] 2 Sam. i. 18.   [53] *Ant.* x. 78.

[54] 2 Chron. xxxv. 25.   [55] Exodus xv.   [56] *Ant.* ii. 346.

[57] *Ant.* i. 17, x. 218 (μήτε προστιθεὶς τοῖς πράγμασιν αὐτὸς ἰδίᾳ).

[58] *e.g.* Edersheim, art. Josephus, in the *Dict. of Christian Biography*, and Bloch, *Die Quellen des Fl. Josephus*, pp. 22–53.

As illustrations of what should, I suppose, be described as
Haggadah, we may take a few instances where Josephus agrees with
the *Book of Jubilees,* one of the earliest works of this class, dating
from a century before our era. In common with *Jubilees,* he tells
us that the beasts in Paradise spoke with human tongue;[59] that
Adam and Eve had daughters;[60] of the inscriptions on pillars made
by the antediluvians to ensure the preservation of their discoveries; [61]
that the name of Pharaoh's daughter, the foster-mother of Moses,
was Thermuthis.[62]

The identification of persons or dates and other inferences deduced
from a comparison of Biblical passages are characteristically
Rabbinic. It was Nimrod, the city-builder, who designed the Tower
of Babel; [63] one anonymous prophet who denounced Jeroboam was
named Ἰάδων,[64] another who foretold Ahab's death because he
spared Benhadad was Micaiah; [65] the man who drew a bow at a
venture and slew him was Ἄμανος,[66] possibly meaning Naaman;
the woman who besought Elisha to save her from her creditors was
the widow of Obadiah, who, in order to support the prophets in
hiding, had resorted to money-lenders.[67] Moses, according to
Josephus,[68] died on the first of the month Adar, according to
Rabbinical tradition on the seventh; [69] and so on.

Around the lawgiver in particular there grew up a rich crop of
legend, both among friends and foes. The *contra Apionem* gives
us the inventions of the enemies of Judaism, representing Moses as
the leper expelled with his band of lepers from Egypt: in the
Antiquities we have the reverse picture. Tales here given of the

[59] *Ant.* i. 41: *Jub.* iii. 28.

[60] *Ant.* i. 52: *Jub.* iv. 1 and 8 (giving names).   [61] *Ant.* i. 70: cf. *Jub.* viii. 3.

[62] *Ant.* ii. 224: *Jub.* xlvii. 5, Tharmuth. The Talmud calls her Bathia and other
names are given elsewhere, Bloch, *op. cit.* 35.

[63] *Ant.* i. 113 f.

[64] *Ant.* viii. 231: has this arisen out of the LXX καὶ ἰδοὺ ἄνθρωπος τοῦ θεοῦ
(3 Regn. xiii. 1)?

[65] *ib.* viii. 391.   [66] *ib.* viii. 414.   [67] *ib.* ix. 47.

[68] *ib.* iv. 327.   [69] *Kiddushin* 38, *Megilla* 13.

infant prodigy find partial parallels in Alexandrian literature. The allusion in Numbers to "the Cushite woman whom he had married "[70] gave rise to stories of his leadership in an Ethiopian campaign, which take various forms in Josephus, the Alexandrian Artapanus and Rabbinical writers. In the account of his end, as I have mentioned, the author has not scrupled to draw upon descriptions of the "passing" of the founders of the Roman race, Aeneas and Romulus.

In his interpretation of the laws—the sphere of *Halakah*, or, as he would say τὰ νόμιμα[71]—Josephus has points of contact with the Palestinians on which I cannot dwell. But the most striking of such interpretations is purely Alexandrian and alien to the spirit of the O. T.: "Our legislator has expressly forbidden us to deride or blaspheme the gods recognised by others, out of respect for the very word 'God'"[72] This is based on the LXX use of the plural θεούς in Ex. xxii. 28 "Thou shalt not revile Elohim"; or perhaps drawn directly from Philo[73] who gives the same interpretation and the same reason for the injunction—the hallowing of the Name.

This brings me to some other indications which have been traced[74] of an acquaintance of Josephus with the writings of the great Alexandrian. He mentions Philo but once, in a brief notice of the embassy to Caligula which was led by that philosopher to defend the maligned Jews of his native city against the accusations of Apion.[75] But Josephus himself has devoted a large part of his apology for Judaism to the refutation of the slanders of that same opponent; and this bond of union in attacking a common enemy might lead the historian to consult the works of his predecessor. The perusal was

[70] Numb. xii. 1.   [71] *e.g. Vita* 191.

[72] *c. Ap.* ii. 237, *cf. Ant.* iv. 207.

[73] *Vita Mos.* ed. Cohn ii. (26) 205; *De spec. leg.* i. (7) 53.

[74] Siegfried, *Philo von Alexandria* 278–281. I have here made some use of my article " Josephus " in Hastings *D.B.*

[75] *Ant.* xviii. 259 f.

probably slight, the deeper philosophy of Philo being beyond his grasp; but there is enough to show that he had looked into the work *On the Creation* (*De opificio mundi*) and perhaps the *Life of Moses*. The projected work on *Customs and Causes* would probably have revealed further points of contact.

The preface to the *Antiquities* and the opening of the *De opificio mundi* run on parallel lines. Both works raise the question why the Mosaic code is preceded by an account of the Creation. Josephus expects that his readers will ask why his work, intended as a record of laws and events, has so large an element of what he calls "physiology." He explains that Moses, unlike other legislators, whose codes begin with contracts and the rights of man, held it necessary, before laying down his code, to elevate men's minds by setting the highest of examples before them and inducing them to contemplate the nature and actions of God, especially as exhibited in the creation.[76] Philo has a similar exordium, contrasting the procedure of Moses and that of other legislators. Moses did not begin by laying down commands and prohibitions, but opened with a marvellous account of the creation, in order to show the harmony existing between the universe and the law and that the law-abiding man is a true citizen of the world (κοσμοπολίτου).[77] This unanimity between the law and the universe is also emphasized by Josephus.[78] Josephus and Philo both refer to the mythical stories which disfigure the codes of other legislators.

In the same context Josephus admits that allegory, which in Philo plays so large a part, has a place in the interpretation of Scripture, reserving details for his projected work.[79] Of such allegorical explanation he gives us elsewhere one striking instance, in which the tabernacle and its furniture and the various articles in the high priest's dress are explained as symbolical of the universe and its constituent elements.[80] Philo gives a similar interpretation of the

[76] *Ant.* i. 18 ff.   [77] *De opif. mundi* 1, 1–3 (Cohn).
[78] *Ant.* i. 24.   [79] *ib.* i. 24 f.
[80] *ib.* iii. 123, 179–187; *cf. B.J.* v. 217 f.

materials used for the hangings of the tabernacle and the high priest's vestments in the *Life of Moses*.[81] The details are not all identical in the two writers, and this particular form of allegorical explanation appears to have been more widespread, parallels being quoted from the *Midrashim* and even from the Samaritan liturgy; [82] so that direct dependence on Philo is here not definitely established.

Again, Josephus remarks on the strange use of the cardinal number " one " instead of the ordinal in the account of the first day of creation in Gen. i. 5, " And there was evening and there was morning, one day," and again reserves his explanation for his future work. Philo had previously commented on the fact and given his own mystical interpretation in the *De opificio mundi*.[83]

To that same work there is another curious parallel in the *contra Apionem*, both writers being apparently influenced by Greek philosophy. Plato in the *Timaeus* [84] had represented God as employing collaborators in the work of creation. And Philo partially followed him, deducing from the plural in Gen. i. 26 (" Let *us* make man ") that man, being of a mixed nature, both good and bad, required a plurality of δημιουργοί, whereas for the rest of creation—heaven, earth, sea, the beasts and plants—God needed no assistant.[85] Josephus does not venture expressly to countenance this heretical doctrine of the " two powers," so firmly rejected by the Rabbis,[86] and indeed he may be intending to combat both Plato and Philo; but he significantly omits to mention man in the passage in question. " We behold His works," he writes,[87] " the light, the heaven, the earth, the sun, the waters, the reproductive creatures (ζῴων γενέσεις), the sprouting crops. These God created, not with hands, not with

81 *De vita Mosis* iii. 6 (88) and 12 (117 ff.).

82 By J. Weill in Theodore Reinach's *Flavius Josèphe* on *Ant.* iii. 180.

83 *De op. mundi* 9 (35) ἡμέραν οὐχὶ πρώτην, ἀλλὰ μίαν, ἢ λέλεκται διὰ τὴν τοῦ νοητοῦ κόσμου μόνωσιν μοναδικὴν ἔχοντος φύσιν: Jos. *Ant.* i. 29.

84 41 C, 42 E.   85 *De opif. mundi* 24 (72 ff.).

86 For the Rabbinic rejection of the heresy that two powers created the world see Moore, *Judaism* i. 381.

87 *c. Ap.* ii. 192.

toil, *not with assistants of whom He had no need*; He willed it so, and forthwith they were made in all their beauty."

In these passages, then, Josephus comes to some extent under the influence of Alexandrian thought. It is impossible here to review his theology as a whole and to estimate the various factors that have gone to the making of it; and indeed his historical works are not the place in which to look for any connected statement of doctrinal beliefs. Writing in Greek and for Greeks, he naturally and almost necessarily adapts himself to their terminology and modes of thought, as when he employs the impersonal phrase " the Divinity " [88] or writes of Fate or Destiny.[89] But, in large measure, he is in harmony with orthodox Rabbinical Judaism. I can but touch on a few points.

He never published his projected work on the being of God, but here is his brief statement, a sort of paraphrase of the first two commandments, immediately preceding the last passage which I quoted: [90] " The universe is in God's hands; perfect and blessed, self-sufficing and sufficing for all, He is the beginning, the middle,[91] and the end of all things. By His works and bounties He is plainly seen, indeed more manifest than ought else; but His form and magnitude surpass our powers of description. No materials, however costly, are fit to make an image of Him; no art has skill to conceive and represent it. The like of Him we have never seen, we do not imagine, and it is impious to conjecture." Elsewhere,[92] he writes that the lawgiver " persuaded all to look to Him as the author of all blessings... He convinced them that no single action, no secret thought could be hid from Him. He represented Him as One, uncreated [93] and immutable to all eternity; in beauty surpassing all mortal form, made known to us by His power, although the nature of His real being passes knowledge."

---

[88] τὸ θεῖον.   [89] ἡ εἱμαρμένη, τὸ χρεών.   [90] *Ap.* ii. 190 f.
[91] For Rabbinical parallels see Th. Reinach, *in loc.*   [92] *Ap.* ii. 166 f.
[93] ἀγένητον, i.e. not born (like the Greek gods). He is using Philonic phraseology: *de opif. mundi* 2 (7) τὸν μὲν ἀγένητόν τε καὶ ἀΐδιον ἀπεφήναντο (of the κόσμος).

On a future life, the historian, as a Pharisee, believes in a return to bodily existence of the souls of the good. The Pharisaic belief he expresses thus: " All souls are imperishable, but the soul of the good alone passes into another body, while the souls of the wicked suffer eternal punishment ";[94] and elsewhere, " Their belief is that souls have a deathless vigour, and that beneath the earth there are punishments and rewards for those who have been devoted in life to vice or virtue: for the former is prescribed everlasting imprisonment, for the latter facility for return to life." [95] In keeping with this is his statement of general Jewish belief in the *contra Apionem*: [96] " Each individual, relying on the witness of his own conscience and the lawgiver's prophecy, confirmed by the sure testimony of God, is firmly persuaded that to those who observe the laws and, if they must needs die for them, willingly meet death, God has granted to be born again and to receive a better life in turn." [97] Similarly in the speech at Jotapata on the iniquity of suicide,[98] " Know you not that they who depart this life in accordance with the law of nature and repay the loan which they received from God, when He who lent it is pleased to reclaim it, win eternal renown... that their souls, remaining spotless and obedient, are allotted the most holy place in heaven, whence in the revolution of the ages (ἐκ περιτροπῆς αἰώνων) they return to find in chaste bodies a new habitation? But, as for those who have laid mad hands upon themselves, the darker regions of Hades receive their souls."

Of any Messianic beliefs Josephus gives no sign. The sentence, of very doubtful authenticity, in the well-known *testimonium* in the *Antiquities*, " This was the Christ " must be reserved for another lecture. Apart from that, he is silent on a subject, associated by him with risings which had brought his country to ruin and to which it was dangerous to allude. But there are two passages, darkly

---

[94] *B.J.* ii. 163.   [95] *Ant.* xviii. 14.   [96] *Ap.* ii. 218.

[97] ἐκ περιτροπῆς, or, in the light of the fuller phrase in the following passage, " in the revolution (of the ages)."

[98] *B.J.* iii. 374 f.

hinting at the fulfilment of prophecy, which seem to suggest that the author had his private opinions and a presentiment of the downfall of the Roman power and of a possible amelioration of his nation's lot. In one, he writes that from the fulfilment even within his own memory, of many of Balaam's prophecies, one may conjecture that the remainder also will come true.[99] In the other, he refuses to deal with a prophecy of Daniel concerning the stone in Nebuchadnezzar's vision, which is to break the kingdoms in pieces, and refers the curious reader to the text of Scripture.[100]

He is careful to note the fulfilment of prophecy and shows something of Rabbinic casuistry in reconciling predictions seemingly inconsistent.[101] And, although as he says in his statement on the Canon of Scripture, the succession of the old prophets has failed,[102] the gift of prophecy was still in his opinion bestowed on favoured individuals. It was possessed by John Hyrcanus, the Essene Judas, the Pharisee Pollio (or Abtalion) and by the historian himself.[103] For miraculous events in the O. T. narrative he constantly suggests rationalistic explanations; he is here accommodating himself to incredulous heathen readers and to a contemporary canon of historical writing on the treatment of "myth," but seems quite ready to accept such explanations himself. In common with most of his contemporaries he shared the belief in the reality of demoniacal possession.[104]

But it is as apologist, rather than as theologian, that Josephus excels, and I will conclude with a reference to that fine apology for Judaism, from which I have often quoted, the *contra Apionem*. Here, at the close, we have something approaching a connected statement of the writer's religious beliefs, and a glowing defence of the lawgiver and his code, expressed with a sincerity and a zeal

---

[99] *Ant.* iv. 125.   [100] *ib.* x. 210.

[101] In the stories of the two Zedekiahs, the son of Chenaanah and the King of Judah, *Ant.* viii. 407 f., x. 106 f.

[102] *c. Ap.* i. 41.

[103] *Ant.* xiii. 299, 311, xv. 4, *B.J.* iii. 399 ff.

[104] *B.J.* vii. 185, *Ant.* viii. 45-48 (for the contemporary method of exorcism).

for his country's religion unmatched in his other works. In the earlier portion of the treatise he challenges the alleged antiquity of the Greeks, accounts for their silence on Jewish history, adduces an array of external evidence for the antiquity of his own race, and crushes the malignant and absurd fictions circulated by their enemies. But he considers the best defence against these false accusations is to be found in the laws themselves, which he proceeds to summarise. He describes the constitution of Moses as a "theocracy," coining the Greek word apparently himself. The religion of Moses was for the many, not, like Greek philosophy, for a select few. His system of education combined precept and practice; through the weekly lessons all Jews know their Law, under which they live as under a father and master. Their unity of creed results in admirable harmony. "Could God," he writes, "be more worthily honoured than by such a scheme, under which religion is the end and aim of the training of the entire community, the priests are entrusted with the special charge of it, and the whole administration of the state resembles some sacred rite of initiation?"[105] Then he passes in review the various laws, the temple cult (strangely spoken of as if still in being), the equitable treatment of aliens, the humanity of the Law. "We put into practice," he says,[106] "what Greeks regard as visionary ideals, and our discipline which leaves no room for freak or individual caprice in matters of everyday life results in the heroism which we display in face of death. Our Laws have stood the test of time and been widely imitated. Without any seductive bait, the Law has found its way among all mankind. Let each (he adds) reflect on his own country and his own household and he will not disbelieve what I say. Were we not ourselves aware of the excellence of our laws, we should have been impelled to pride ourselves upon them by the multitude of their admirers."

That fine encomium will, I think, fitly close my lecture to-day.

[105] *Ap.* ii. 188.
[106] I here summarize the admirable peroration which should be read in full.

7*

JOSEPHUS AND HELLENISM:
HIS GREEK ASSISTANTS

I spoke yesterday of Josephus in his relation to the religion of his race, as priest and Rabbi, exponent of the Scriptures and of the theology and traditional lore of Judaism. To-day I turn to consider him in another aspect, as the Hellenist, trained in all the riches of Greek learning. But with him I would here associate others to whom he is immensely indebted. We hear much from our author of his own achievements: we hear little of those skilled and assiduous helpers in the background, who were no mere amanuenses, but polished his periods, occasionally took over the composition of large portions of the narrative, and hunted up, made extracts from, and translated into elegant Greek, edicts, acts, and other relevant records written in crabbed Latin characters and deposited in the imperial archives in the Roman Capitol. These anonymous menials deserve recognition for their invaluable services, and, in considering our author as Hellenist, instead of leaving him in solitary grandeur, we should do them justice by speaking of " Josephus and Co."

You may perhaps be familiar with some old rhymes with regard to an eminent Master of Balliol College, Oxford, who is said to have had a good deal of spade-work done for him by his assistant Tutors and to have made scanty acknowledgment:—

> "I'm the head: my name is Jowett,
> What is to be known I know it,
> What I know not is not knowledge;
> I'm the Master of this College."

And then the Tutor puts in his claim:—

> "Oh, I say, my name is Forbes,
> But the Master me absorbs—
> Me and many other 'mes'
> In his big Thucydides."

Far be it from me to compare the Rev. Dr. Benjamin Jowett with Flavius Josephus, but the assistants of the latter might with better reason have made a similar protest.

The historian's literary career opened with a narrative of the Jewish War written in his native Aramaic or, as some think, Hebrew, for an Eastern audience. But that medium was soon discarded. His extant works are all addressed to Graeco-Roman readers, and for that wider circle a thorough mastery of Greek was essential. His life in Palestine in that period of turmoil, culminating in the Great War, would afford little opportunity for such study.   True, it was a bilingual country, but the vernacular Greek there spoken was ill suited for works addressed to cultivated and fastidious readers.   Our author's "hard training and laborious exercises" [1] in his student days were devoted to the investigation of the tenets of the rival sects of his nation, nor, we may be sure, did his three years residence in the hermitage of Bannus include a course in Thucydides.   The mastery of Greek displayed in his writings must have been wholly acquired in Rome.

The Jewish Dispersion at all times produced accomplished linguists, though the foreign tongue was by some assimilated with difficulty and their native Aramaic left an occasional mark on their Greek syntax. The pioneers who produced the first Greek version of the Scriptures at Alexandria performed a remarkable feat; it is true they wrote for the people in the vernacular, not the literary, Greek, and were moreover hampered by their task as translators and by their reverence for the letter of the inspired original, which accounts for their retention of some Hebrew phraseology.   The thorough command of the language of which Alexandrian writers, free from such restrictions, were capable, is seen to perfection in the book of Wisdom or the works of Philo.

But Alexandria was the university of Greek learning, and the Alexandrian Jew, who had forgotten his Aramaic, was acquainted

[1] *Vita* 11.

with a smattering of Greek from his infancy. At Rome the Palestinian Josephus had almost to start from the beginning and to master the grammar, before immersing himself in those masses of literature which were to serve alike as the materials for his history and as his models of style. He clearly took immense pains to acquire a good style and, though his work is very unequal, portions of it attain a remarkably high level. No trace of his native Aramaic is allowed to sully the pages of the Greek version of his *Jewish War*, and the one trace of Semitism thought to have been discovered elsewhere proves illusory.[2] He must further endeavour fastidiously to abjure the "vulgarisms" of the later Alexandrian speech, which were not disdained even by such a writer as Polybius.

This command of the language was, however, as I said, not wholly his own, and I propose in this lecture to go in quest of some of his assistants. It will be a study in diversities of style. Such a study, taking us back as it were into the *scriptorium* of an ancient writer and disclosing something of his methods, is not without its human interest. I have elsewhere shown [3] how variations in style may be detected in the Greek Bible, and how the different renderings of such a common phrase as "Thus saith the Lord" and other changes of style, which make their appearance after the middle of a book of the LXX suggest that the Alexandrian translators of some of the prophetical books worked in pairs, and, to expedite their labours, bisected the particular book upon which they were engaged and alternately dictated and translated the Hebrew. In the New Testament we know the name of one of S. Paul's amanuenses,[4] and the names of others have been plausibly conjectured;[5] variations in the style of some of the Pauline Epistles have been thought to be traceable to the employment of various

[2] The use of the verb προστίθεσθαι to express "again," Schmidt, *De Flav. Josephi elocutione* (1893) 516, with an article in the *Journal of Theol. Studies*, July 1929.

[3] *The Septuagint and Jewish Worship*, Lecture I.

[4] "I, Tertius, who write the epistle, salute you," Rom. xvi. 22.

[5] Burkitt, *Christian Beginnings* 131 ff.

amanuenses. But in the case of Josephus we are not left merely to conjecture: we have his own admission that he employed assistants.

Two passages may first be quoted, in which the author alludes to his literary qualifications and his appreciation of the value of style. Here is his estimate of his own attainments which he makes at the close of the *Antiquities*.[6] There is little modesty about it, though it does contain one significant admission about his pronunciation of Greek, in apology it would seem to those who had heard his attempts to speak the language. "I make bold to say that no one else, whether Jew or alien, could with the best will in the world have produced a work of such accuracy as this for Greek readers. For my countrymen admit that I am easily pre-eminent among them in the lore of my native land; and I have moreover striven to acquaint myself with Greek literature (some MSS add 'including poetry,' καὶ ποιητικῶν μαθημάτων) and am proficient in the grammar, although long habituation to my native tongue has prevented me from acquiring the correct pronunciation." That little addition in some MSS, "and poetical learning," is intriguing. It is quite possible to account for the accidental omission of the words by what is called *homoioteleuton* ("like-ending"); on the other hand, as will appear, one of the author's assistants was a keen lover of the Greek dramatists, and my friend Dr. Eisler suggests that it is he who, knowing the truth about these boasted achievements of his master, has deliberately erased the words from a later edition. Here again is a passage on the virtue of style at the opening of Book xiv, written when the author was wearying of his task and was soon to entrust it to other hands:[7] "Among other qualifications the historian and reporter of events, which owing to their antiquity are unfamiliar to most men, needs the charm of style, in so far as this is attainable by the choice and nice adjustment (ἁρμονία) of words and by whatever else may serve to embellish the narrative, in order that the reader, along with

[6] *Ant.* xx. 262 ff.   [7] *ib.* xiv. 2.

instruction, may find a certain fascination and delight." By the " nice adjustment " or " harmony " of words he refers to the avoidance of hiatus (or clashing of vowels): the rule that a word ending with a vowel must not collide with an initial vowel of the next is studiously observed throughout a large portion of his work— a very exacting requirement.

Turning to our author's earliest and greatest work, we find, as I have said, that the *Jewish War* possesses extraordinary merits. The style is an excellent specimen of the Atticistic Greek of the first century, modelled on, if not quite on a level with, that of the great masters of the age of Pericles. A choice vocabulary, well knit sentences and paragraphs, niceties in the use of particles and the order of words, a uniformly classical style without slavish imitation of classical models—these and other excellences combine to give the work high rank in Greek literature.

This thorough command of the intricacies and niceties of the Greek language in an author who had hitherto written only in Aramaic would be astounding, were it not for an *obiter dictum* in a later work. In the *contra Apionem* written about a quarter of a century after the *War*, the historian makes a tardy acknowledgment of the help received by him in the composition of the earlier work. He employed, he tells us, certain collaborators for the sake of the Greek (χρησάμενός τισι πρὸς τὴν Ἑλληνίδα φωνὴν συνεργοῖς).[8]

The modern editor is grateful for this illuminating acknowledgment and can afford to forgive its tardiness. The assistants concerned may well have complained that it was not made before, and indeed it is possible that, like other admissions in his later works ("matters about which I have hitherto kept silence" as he says),[9] it was extorted from him by expostulation. It is true that ancient works had no exact counterpart to the modern preface, that convenient receptable for due acknowledgment of indebtedness

[8] *Ap.* i. 50.
[9] *Vita* 338.

and other personal matters.   But the *Jewish War* does include a
full proem, in which the author has said a good deal about himself.
A word of graceful and timely acknowledgment would not have
been out of place here; instead of this the only allusion there made
to " erudite Greeks " is a severe censure for their disregard of
historical accuracy.   The assistants indeed had a thankless taskmaster.
That they were at least well remunerated out of the author's pension
may, I hope, be inferred from a remark in his proem: " For myself,
at a vast expenditure of *money* and pains, I, a foreigner, present
to Greeks and Romans this memorial of great achievements." [10]
Their names and social status are unrecorded.   Their culture and
recondite knowledge of Greek literature led me at first to think of
them as the author's " literary friends in Rome "; but we should
perhaps be more correct in regarding them as his slaves, like that
eunuch slave who was tutor (παιδαγωγός) to the historian's son and
was punished by Domitian's orders for defaming his master.[11]
Josephus had foes in his own household.

At any rate the immense debt which the author of the *Jewish
War* owes to these admirable assistants is apparent on almost every
page.   Among other excellences, the work contains a large and
choice vocabulary—not confined to military terms—peculiar to
itself, or but rarely represented in certain parts of the *Antiquities*.
The last book (vii) stands apart: here another vocabulary, characteristic of the *Antiquities,* makes its appearance.   It would seem
that the author at the close of his task has been thrown more upon
his own resources, though here too indications of assistance are not
wanting.   The last book of a literary work was liable to escape
revision, and, though different causes probably came into play, it is
curious to recall that the last book of Thucydides similarly stands
apart from the rest: as has often been remarked it seems to have
lacked the author's final touches.   Some marks of the author's own
style also appear at an earlier point, in the narrative of his youthful career in Galilee at the end of Book ii.

[10] *B.J.* i. 16.   [11] *Vita* 429.

Josephus mentions συνεργοί in the plural. I have not so far succeeded in discriminating the respective contributions of the two or more members of his literary staff employed on the *War*. The detection of two of his main assistants comes only in the later work, the *Antiquities,* to which I now turn. There is no allusion to any help having been obtained here, but the collaborators have left their own indelible impress upon the text.

The short proem to the *Antiquities* contains an interesting personal statement concerning the genesis of the author's *magnum opus,* with some human touches on his shrinking from the formidable task which he had undertaken and the encouragement of his patrons which alone enabled him to carry it to completion. He tells us [12] how originally, when he wrote the *Jewish War,* he had contemplated a single comprehensive work, to embrace in addition to the narrative of the recent campaign the whole history of his nation, but how, realizing the unwieldy compass of such a work, he decided to divide it into two. Yet even so the writing of the *Archaeology,* the complete history of the race, proved an appalling task. "As time went on," he writes, and historians of all ages would sympathize with his feelings, "as is wont to happen to those who design to handle large themes, I was beset by hesitation and delay in presenting so vast a subject in a foreign and strange tongue. However, there were certain persons who wished for the history and instigated me to pursue it, and above all Epaphroditus," &c.

"There was hesitation and delay." The phrase, like so many, is reminiscent of a favourite model, Thucydides, and of the most well-thumbed portion of his work, the Syracusan expedition,[13] but expresses a verifiable fact. It is possible, I think, to lay a finger on one point where the work was laid down and probably abandoned for a season. That point is the end of Book xiv, where the narrative has just reached the capture of Jerusalem by Herod and Sossius in the year 37 B.C. and Herod the Great has just come into the kingdom conferred on him three years earlier in Rome.

[12] *Ant.* i. 6-8.   [13] Thuc. vii. 49. 4.

At this point the narrative undergoes a marked transformation. Just before it we may detect, if I am not mistaken, an indication of weariness; just after it begins a new manner of dealing with the author's materials, accompanied by a change of style. These changes persist for nearly five books. I infer that the work has been entrusted to other hands. The "weariness" of which I spoke betrays itself in the repeated use of old materials. The author has now reached a period which he has previously covered: the story of the rise of Antipater and Herod, which is the subject of Book xiv of the *Antiquities*, has already been graphically told in the *Jewish War*. He has some new materials at his disposal, but is mainly still dependent on his old source, Nicolas of Damascus. Now, while it was customary for ancient historians to make free and unacknowledged use of the published work of their predecessors, without any sense of what we should call "plagiarism," it was almost a point of honour with them to vary the phraseology. Still more did this rule apply where the writer was twice covering the same ground: he must not "plagiarise" from himself. Even a speech delivered on a particular occasion must, if reduplicated, be reported in different language. Now, Josephus, who is usually scrupulous in this matter, at the end of book xiv of the *Antiquities*, contrary to his wont, gives us an account of Herod's capture of Jerusalem which is almost a *verbatim* repetition of that already given in the *Jewish War*. He is beginning to repeat himself or rather to transcribe afresh his old authority, Nicolas. For some time the two narratives have been running so closely parallel as to make the minor changes significant and purposeful; and it is not accidental that Laqueur selects just this fourteenth book for a detailed analysis and comparison of the different points of view presented. He could not have done the same for Book xv. Here the narrative has been completely recast and amplified by recourse to Nicolas and by the incorporation of new matter, and whereas in the *War* the external history of Herod's reign has been kept distinct from the domestic tragedies, in the *Antiquities* the events are presented in chronological order.

This change of treatment is, as I said, accompanied by a change, or rather changes, of style, extending from the opening of Book xv to near the end of Book xix.[14] Towards the end of Book xix there is a return to what may be called the "normal" style, which continues to the end of the work (Book xx) and on into its appendix, the *curriculum vitae*. The author, approaching the end of his task, apparently once more takes the pen into his own hands.

This long section, compiled largely or wholly by others, occupies some five books or about a quarter of the whole work, and covers a period of 78 years from the establishment on his throne of Herod the Great in the year 37 B.C. to the confirmation of Agrippa I in his kingdom by Claudius in the year 41 A.D. It is the period which to some of us appears the greatest in the world's history, that immediately preceding and following the opening of the Christian era; and it is remarkable that the extraneous composition includes the famous *testimonium Flavianum* on Jesus Christ.

The peculiarities of this portion cannot be referred to the author himself. Some variation in an author's style might not be unnatural in a work laid by for a considerable time. But a writer does not change his style two or three times over, nor suddenly lapse for a time into patent and unmistakable mannerisms such as we find in three of these books. For the extraneous section in which these abnormalities occur falls into two smaller portions. Books xv and xvi bear the marks of an able assistant, such as those employed in the *War*; while Books xvii–xix betray the idiosyncrasies and pedantic tricks of a hack, an imitator of Thucydides.

Nor again, as might be thought, are the peculiarities attributable to the author's use of different authorities. For the long narrative of Herod's reign begins in Book xiv in the "normal" style, extends right through the more elegantly written books xv and xvi, and ends in the extravagant phraseology of xvii. The main source throughout is doubtless Nicolas; yet the variation in style cuts this connected episode into three, and one pen after another takes up

[14] To xix. 275 (or 277).

the poignant tale. Again, the work of Nicolas ceases with the accession of Archelaus in the middle of Book xvii; and while the second assistant begins with Herod the Great and his successor, he ends in xix with Roman history and the assassination of Caligula, obviously drawn from quite a different (Latin) source. Yet the same blatant mannerisms pervade this whole section (xvii–xix) from beginning to end.

We may speculate on the reasons which induced Josephus to seek such liberal aid at this particular point. A main cause was doubtless that weariness, hesitation and difficulty of coping with an acquired tongue, to which he alludes in his proem. But we can imagine others. He had reached a period already partially covered, also with assistance, in the *War*: he was content to leave the reproduction of the sequel to others, with instructions to reshape the materials and vary the phraseology. But, over and above the old documents, he had now found fresh matter to incorporate and much of it was in *Latin*. For a large part of Book xviii and nearly the whole of xix the scene shifts from Palestine to Rome, and, though much of the narrative has but a remote bearing on Jewish history, it becomes an authority of the first rank for the court history of the successors of Augustus. The varying fortunes of Agrippa I in Rome are the peg on which is hung an interesting disquisition on the dilatory policy of Tiberius and the fullest extant account of the murder of Caligula and the accession of Claudius. Here the author is doubtless dependent on Latin sources, and, if Greek always remained to him a foreign tongue, his proficiency in Latin was even slighter. He needed a helper to translate those documents in cursive Roman characters in the imperial archives or other Latin literary works.

We are then, I think, justified in regarding these two contiguous portions, books xv–xvi and xvii–xix, as the work of a pair of assistants, whom, for lack of names, I will call respectively α and β.

I will consider the latter first, because the characteristics of his style are patent and cannot fail to strike a reader's eye. A student who happened to make his first acquaintance with Josephus in this portion would pronounce him a difficult writer and perhaps be deterred by the involved and turgid language, whereas he would find the *Life* absurdly easy and crude. The distinctive features of the writer of xvii–xix are (1) free plagiarism from Thucydides and (2) certain mannerisms of his own, in which he seems to be trying his hand at imitating, without actually copying, his great model. He may be called the Thucydidean hack.

Thucydides was the natural standard of historical style, and a restrained use of his phraseology—an occasional reminiscence, such as we find in the *Jewish War*—was quite legitimate. When we turn to the *Antiquities* the parallels become more abundant and reach their climax in these books xvii–xix, where the writer in every paragraph quarries freely from this mine. He may also, as I hope to show, be held responsible for some of the parallels in the earlier books.

The "Thucydideans," as they are called, were a notorious tribe in the days of Josephus. A generation or two before his time we find them ridiculed by Cicero, a generation after him by Lucian. Cicero's satire [15] is directed against the rhetoricians who frame their speeches on the model of the great Athenian. "See," he says, "there are some who profess themselves Thucydideans, a new and unheard of class of ignoramuses ... Their speeches have so many obscure and recondite sentences that they can scarce be understood," and so on. Lucian in his excellent little treatise on "How history should be written," [16] containing sound advice not only for the historian but for the modern lecturer, makes sport of the imitators of the Athenian, who pompously open their works with their own outlandish names —"Crepereus Calpurnianus the Pompeiopolitan wrote the history of the war in which the Parthians and the Romans fought against one another, beginning to write when they first took up arms"— and who fill their pages with "little rags" (μικρὰ ῥάκια) from their model. After listening to one of these ranters declaiming his work,

---

[15] *Orator* ix. 30. I owe the reference to Drüner (n. 17).

[16] *Quomodo hist. sit conscribenda* 15 (21–23).

he says "I left him burying the unfortunate Athenians in Nisibis, knowing exactly what he would say on my departure."

Just so it may be said that in portions of the *Antiquities*, and in these three books in particular, the old Grecian battles are refought, the orations of Pericles redelivered, on Palestinian or Italian soil. The whole history of the Peloponnesian war is at the writer's finger ends, but the retreat from Syracuse, the siege of Plataea and the speeches of Pericles provide the most numerous reminiscences.[17]

A few instances of "Thucydideanisms" and other tricks of style must suffice. This journalistic hack is verbose and prefers two or more words to one. Periphrasis is frequent and the double negative —"not incapable of," "not averse from"—a special favourite. Thucydides had once used the former phrase in a character sketch of Themistocles "who even in matters in which he had no experience was not incapable of (οὐκ ἀπήλλακτο) forming a sufficient judgment."[18] The writer of *Ant.* xvii–xix uses the phrase, found nowhere else in Josephus, some 15 times, once with obvious dependence on the Thucydides passage.[19] After the assassination of Caligula in the underground passage still shown to visitors to the Palatine in Rome, Claudius was found in hiding and carried off by the Roman troops as their emperor. "One of the soldiers," I translate literally, "being unskilled to make sure of the features because of the darkness, but not incapable of being a judge that the skulking figure was a man." That illustrates the cumbrous pedantry of the scribe: "being unskilled" for "unable," "not incapable" and the resolution of the simple verb κρίνειν ("judge") of Thucydides into κριτὴς εἶναι ("be a judge"). For "not incapable" we have the variation "not averse from" (οὐκ ἀποτετραμμένος) i. e. "ready" (to do something), also confined to this hack. If there is one word demanding brevity it is surely "quickly," especially when used with an imperative; but our scribe often employs seven. The source of

---

[17] A long, but not quite exhaustive, list is given by Drüner, *Untersuchungen über Josephus,* 1896.

[18] Thuc. i. 138.   [19] *Ant.* xix. 217.

this particular periphrasis is again literary. In Thucydides,[20] Nicias in straits in Sicily sends an urgent request to Athens for reinforcements, "But do whatever you mean to do at the very beginning of spring and let there be no delay" (εὐθὺς καὶ μὴ ἐς ἀναβολὰς πράσσετε). This phrase οὐδὲν (μηδὲν) εἰς ἀναβολάς, usually strengthened by ἀλλ᾽ ἐκ τοῦ ὀξέος ("but off the reel" as we might say), occurs a dozen times in this part of Josephus, and only once in an earlier book,[21] where I have no doubt that the same hand has been at work. In the account of the plague of Athens Thucydides tells us that the stricken died in solitude, abandoned by their friends; or, if they ventured to attend them, they perished, "especially those who aspired to heroism" (οἱ ἀρετῆς τι μεταποιούμενοι).[22] This phrase "aspiring to heroism" has caught the fancy of the amanuensis who rings the changes upon it.[23] And so we might go on. The departure from the author's normal practice even extends to the spelling: the double σ (of Thucydides) in words like πράσσειν replaces the so-called "Attic" double τ (πράττειν), elsewhere usual in Josephus. Among other peculiarities of this assistant may be mentioned ἡδονῇ δέχεσθαι "receive with pleasure" (important from its occurrence in the *testimonium Flavianum*),[24] the longer form of the relative pronoun, ὁπόσος for the usual ὅσος (a hall-mark of this hack who uses it over a 100 times, often without verb, as in καὶ ὁπόσα ἐχόμενα "and whatever is akin" = "and the like"), συνέρχεσθαι in the sense of "happen," μεθιστάναι or μεταχειρίζεσθαι "remove" instead of "kill," the Ionic ἁμαρτάς for ἁμαρτία. The commonplace word is studiously shunned and replaced by the unusual and *bizarre*. The writer had the faults of the inferior journalist.

The cult of Thucydides was, as I said, in fashion: his devotees formed a clique like the Browningites or the Meredithians of modern

---

[20] vii. 15.   [21] *Ant.* vii. 224.   [22] Thuc. ii. 51.

[23] ἀρετῆς μεταποιεῖσθαι *Ant.* xviii. 20, 278, ὀριγνᾶσθαι xvii. 153, προσποίησις xvii. 149, 181; *cf.* μεταποίησις iii. 58, ἀντιποίησις iv. 154.

[24] *Ant.* xviii. 6, 59, 63, 70, 236, 333; xix. 127, 185; also ἡδονῇ φέρειν xvii. 148, &c.

days. If we seek for further reasons for this writer's whimsicalities, we may perhaps name two. In the earlier portion of his work, the account of the latter days of Herod the Great in Book xvii, we have merely a verbose paraphrase of the previous narrative in the *War*: there has been no such recourse to the original authority, Nicolas, as we find in Books xv–xvi. The amanuensis here must have received instructions from his "boss" (if that colloquialism may be used of the great historian) "Take the *War* as your authority, but be careful to vary the phraseology." This gave the scribe free rein to indulge his natural propensities. But I cannot help thinking that there may have been another more malicious incentive. Invited to become a partner in an important literary undertaking, for which his employer was to take the sole credit, and given a free hand in the phraseology, he was determined to leave his own mark, if not his name, upon his handiwork, and he has successfully done so.

That this Thucydidean is thus responsible for writing practically the whole of Books xvii–xix appears unquestionable: his speech bewrays him. But, as I said, imitation of Thucydides is not confined to this portion, though here it reaches a climax. The question then arises, did this secretary lend occasional aid elsewhere? I think he did, and that where we find in earlier portions of the *Antiquities* an accumulation of Thucydidean phrases, especially if they are among the favourite phrases in Books xvii–xix and moreover occur in conjunction with some known mannerism, there the same hand has been at work. He has not yet fully developed those later mannerisms, but we can already detect one or two of them in embryo. I have mentioned his cumbrous seven-word periphrasis of "forthwith," repeated a dozen times in *Ant.* xvii–xix. To this we find one parallel in an earlier book,[25] in the description of the despatch of messengers from Jerusalem to report Absalom's plans to David outside the city, where we read (in a literal translation) "and they deferred nothing to delays and procrastination," i.e. "they departed post-haste." Here we may well suspect the hand

[25] *Ant.* vii. 224.

Thackeray.   8

of the hack. Still more significant is the account of the destruction by fire of Korah and all his company, because here we find not only express imitation of Thucydides, but also one of this scribe's most distinctive marks, the use of the pronoun ὁπόσος for ὅσος, of which there are 100 instances in *Ant.* xvii–xix and only four elsewhere. You may remember how in the Peloponnesian War the besiegers of Plataea attempted to destroy the city by a huge bonfire. "A flame arose," writes Thucydides,[26] "of which the like had never before been made by the hand of man"; and then, with characteristic avoidance of exaggeration and an allusion to an ancient belief, he adds "I am not speaking of fires in the mountains, when the woods have spontaneously blazed up from the action of the wind and mutual attrition." The Plataean bonfire fell short of those mighty forest-fires. Well, our writer can better that: he must have a blaze that will "lick creation." Here is his picture:[27] "And Aaron and Korah, with his 250 followers, came forth, and they all offered incense in the censers which (ὁπόσα) they had brought. And suddenly there blazed up a fire, the like of which had never in the records of history been made by the hand of man, nor was ever ejected from the earth through subterranean current of heat,[28] nor yet spontaneously broke out in the woods from the violence of the wind and mutual attrition."

From these and a few similar passages we may infer that, besides taking over the large portion towards the close, the Thucydidean has been requisitioned to impart some purple patches to the earlier narrative.

The pilferer of whom I have been speaking has thus left his indelible impression. The thumb-marks are there and it needs no Sherlock Holmes to detect them. The handiwork of his fellow, a man of a distinctly superior type, was not so easily discoverable,

---

[26] ii. 77 (Jowett).   [27] *Ant.* iv. 54 f.

[28] The eruption of Vesuvius in 79 A.D., which buried Pompeii and Herculaneum, is doubtless here in mind—it is mentioned in *Ant.* xx. 144.

and a personal allusion to the circumstances which brought me upon his tracks will, I hope, be forgiven.

Many years ago, I began collecting materials for a *Josephus Lexicon*, which, thanks to the munificence of the *Kohut Memorial Foundation*, is now on the way to publication. I began with a limited portion, the last five books of the *Antiquities*. My immediate object was to collect and classify all peculiarities of the Thucydidean assistant and to fix the precise limits of his work. I knew the approximate limits (Books xvii–xix), but it was necessary to include, as a contrast, some portions of what I regarded as the "normal" style on either side of this, viz. Book xvi on the one side and Book xx on the other. I was not, I think, mistaken in regarding Book xx as written in the "normal" style of our author; here and in the appended *Life* we get as near as we can anywhere to the *ipsissima verba* of Josephus. But I was, as it proved, mistaken in regarding Book xvi as also in the "normal" style. I had unwittingly started my investigation in the middle of the work of a second assistant. It was not until I extended my researches to the whole of the *Antiquities* that I became aware of this. I then found that Books xv and xvi were linked by a special vocabulary and numerous small niceties of style, which were either peculiar to these books or only to be paralleled in certain parts of the *Jewish War*: I was on the track of a second associate. Josephus had wearily laid down his pen at the end of Book xiv, and for the next five books employed successive assistants, responsible for two and for three books respectively.

This first assistant ("α") excelled the other ("β"), and Josephus was fortunate in securing his services. As before, the criteria are two: certain distinctive characteristics of style, and an affinity to a particular class of Greek literature. But here instead of "mannerisms" I should speak of "niceties" and instead of "plagiarism" of "felicitous reminiscences" of a cultivated mind. I need not trouble you with the various subtle delicacies of style and vocabulary which first put me on the track of this assistant,

8*

and will confine myself to his echoes of classical masterpieces. He was evidently well-versed in Greek literature as a whole and does not disdain an incidental reminiscence of Thucydides: but his distinctive characteristic is a love of Greek poetry, Sophocles in particular. Now Thucydides was a natural quarry for the hack historian, but Sophocles is perhaps the last model to which one would expect a Jewish annalist to turn. The occasional, unsought echoes of that most charming of Greek poets, which we here find, bespeak an instinctive literary taste. Whether the plays of Sophocles were acted in the Roman theatres I do not know; but this writer had clearly read them, especially the *Ajax* and the *Electra*, *con amore*. It is hard to believe that he was a slave. It is but a word or phrase inserted unobtrusively here and there, but their source is unmistakable. In Book xv of the *Antiquities* we find parallels to the *Ajax*, in the phrase ἀπὸ τοῦ στέγους διοπτεύειν [29] of the dizzy spectacle from the roof of Herod's palace into the ravine below (after *Aj.* 307 διοπτεύει στέγος), a little below [30] κατὰ δ᾽ ἡλίου βολάς "towards the sunbeams" i. e. "on the east" (after *Aj.* 877) and higher up the word ἐνώμοτος.[31] From the Electra we find in *Ant.* xvi the phrases ποῖ ποτ᾽ οἴχονταί σου . . . αἱ φρένες,[32] "Whither have your wits gone?" in the mouth of the old soldier Tiro expostulating with Herod (after *El.* 390 ποῖ ποτ᾽ εἶ φρενῶν;) and μῖσος ἐντετηκέναι[33] of hatred melting or sinking deep into the soul (after *El.* 1311). In all we find about a dozen echoes of the Athenian tragedian concentrated into these two books.[34]

It is true that the parallels are not wholly confined to these books. But these Sophoclean reminiscences, taken in connexion with certain niceties of style, are the clue which reveal the activity of this assistant in other parts of the work. The results which emerge are, first, that the poet-lover, like the Thucydidean, has, besides taking over the composition of one large section of the

[29] *Ant.* xv. 412.   [30] *ib.* 418.   [31] *ib.* 368: *Aj.* 1113.   [32] *Ant.* xvi. 380.
[33] *ib.* 93.   [34] *e. g.* the words δεξίωμα, δυσγένεια, προσαρκεῖν, &c.

Antiquities, lent occasional aid elsewhere, and, secondly, that he was one of the first-rate assistants employed on the earlier work, the *Jewish War*. When we find in the *War* reminiscences of the *same plays* of Sophocles as those from which the phrases in the *Antiquities* are derived, we may be sure that the same hand has been at work. No such parallels occur in *Ant.* xvii–xix, nor did the Thucydidean take any part in the writing of the *Jewish War*; his services were only employed for the historian's later work.

Reminiscences of Sophocles are specially frequent in the third book of the *War*. From the writer's favourite play, the *Electra*, we have the phrases θράσος ὁπλίζειν of the Jews "armed by recklessness,"[35] ἀφειδεῖν ψυχῆς "to be prodigal of life"[36] and what I take to be a paraphrase of a familiar line in the same context of that play[37] put into the mouth of Titus, possibly, as I have suggested in a previous lecture,[38] as a delicate compliment to his classical taste. From the *Philoctetes* we have οὐδὲν ὑγιὲς φρονεῖν,[39] from the *Trachiniae* θάρσος προξενεῖν "afford confidence"[40] and ζῇ καὶ τέθηλε "live and flourish."[41]

From the same hand doubtless come some sporadic allusions to Euripides. I will mention but two which occur in earlier portions of the *Antiquities*. Hagar fleeing from Sarah with the infant Ishmael, when water fails, lays the child at his last gasp under a pine tree and wanders further on that he may not expire in her presence (θεῖσα τὸ παιδίον ψυχορραγοῦν, ὡς μὴ παρούσης τὴν ψυχὴν ἀφῇ, προίει).[42] Here we have an obvious reminiscence of the *Hercules Furens* 324 f., where Amphitryon says, "Kill me and my wife first, that we may not see those children ... at their

---

[35] *B.J.* iii. 153: Soph., *El.* 995 f.

[36] *B.J.* iii. 212, *El.* 980.

[37] *B.J.* iii. 495: *El.* 945 ὅρα πόνου τοι χωρὶς οὐδὲν εὐτυχεῖ.

[38] p. 43.

[39] *B.J.* v. 326, *Ant.* ix. 118; *Phil.* 1006.

[40] *B.J.* v. 66: *Trach.* 726.

[41] *B.J.* vii. 348: *Trach.* 235.

[42] *Ant.* i. 218.

last gasp and calling upon their mother (ὡς μὴ τέκν' εἰσίδωμεν...
ψυχορραγοῦντα καὶ καλοῦντα μητέρα). Josephus is not the place
where we should look for an allusion to a *lost* play of Euripides;
yet such may be found. Stobaeus has preserved a fragment of the
Ino of that poet:—[43]

> "When blest by fortune slack not every rein:
> When faring ill hold fast to kindly hope"
>
> (... κακῶς τε πράσσουσ' ἐλπίδος κεδνῆς ἔχου).

Of this we have a clear echo when we read of Aristobulus, after his
defeat by Pompey, that "though faring ill he none the less held fast
to good hope" (καὶ πράττων κακῶς οὐδὲν ἧττον ἐλπίδος ἀγαθῆς
εἴχετο).[44]

Beside these parallels with Greek poetry, there are not wanting
echoes of Virgil and other Latin authors. Josephus, we may be sure,
had but a slight acquaintance with Latin literature, and these reminiscences doubtless come from an assistant, probably from the
poet-lover already mentioned. At any rate two of them occur in
the same third book of the *War* which contains the Sophoclean
phrases. The sack of Jotapata recalls the siege of Troy. In consequence of the information of a Jewish deserter that "about the
last watch of the night, at an hour when... jaded men easily
succumb to morning slumber, the sentinels used to drop asleep...
the Romans advanced in silence to the walls. Titus was first to
mount... They cut down the sentries and entered the city." [45] So
in a famous passage in the second Aeneid,[46] where the Greeks issue
from the wooden horse, "Machaon (came) first... They enter the
city buried in sleep and wine, the sentries are cut down... It was
the time when the first rest steals over wearied mortals." Later on
the tale of the fall of Jotapata is carried to Jerusalem by Rumour

---

[43] Dindorf, *Frag.* 407.

[44] *Ant.* xiv. 96; the phrase ἀγαθῆς ἐλπίδος ἔχεσθαι recurs in *Ant.* viii. 214.

[45] *B.J.* iii. 319 ff.   [46] *Aen.* ii. 263 ff.

personified (Φήμη), embroidering facts with fiction,[47] where there is a reminiscence of the Virgilian picture of Fama, who "flew with rumors mixed of false and true." [48]

I would add one more curious instance where Josephus, or rather his assistant, has apparently gone to a Latin prose writer, the historian Sallust, for a picture of a villain. If I am not mistaken, the black portrait drawn of John of Gischala is partly based on the character-sketch of that arch-villain and conspirator in the last days of the Roman republic, Lucius Catiline. Here is the description of John: [49] "While Josephus was thus directing affairs in Galilee, there appeared upon the scene an intriguer, a native of Gischala, named John, son of Levi, the most unscrupulous and crafty of all who have ever gained notoriety by such infamous means. *Poor at the opening of his career*, his penury had long thwarted his malicious designs; a ready liar and clever in obtaining credit for his lies, he made a merit of deceit... Ever full of high ambitions (ἀεὶ μὲν ἐπιθυμήσας μεγάλων), his hopes were fed on the basest of knaveries... He was already aspiring to the command and had yet higher ambitions, but *was checked by impecuniosity*." And here is a slighter sketch of the man elsewhere.[50] "The people of Gischala had been incited to rebel... by John, son of Levi, a charlatan of an extremely subtle character, always ready to indulge great expectations and an adept in realizing them; all knew that he had set his heart on war in order to attain supreme power." Beside these passages I would set the portrait of the Roman conspirator [51] or the main features of it: "Lucius Catiline was of noble birth, of great vigour both of body and mind, but of a depraved genius. From his youth up he revelled in intestine war, murder, rapine, civil discord... An audacious spirit, crafty, subtle, a ready hypocrite and dissimulator on any matter... His monstrous spirit... was ever ambitious of things too high for him (*nimis alta semper cupiebat*)...

[47] *B.J.* iii. 433 f. The passage is quoted on p. 50.
[48] *Aen.* iv. 173 ff. " et pariter facta atque infecta canebat " (tr. Conington).
[49] *B.J.* ii. 585 ff.   [50] *ib.* iv. 85.   [51] Sallust, *de Cat. conjur.* 5.

A burning passion had possessed him to capture the republic, and while seeking a kingdom for himself, he cared not by what means he pursued his ends. His fierce spirit was daily more and more agitated by *lack of money* (*inopia rei familiaris*) and by consciousness of his crimes." There are several minor parallels here, but the allusion to impecuniosity as the barrier to the criminal's nefarious designs clinches, to my mind, the connexion between the two portraits.

If John was in our author's eyes the villain of the tragedy of his nation, the hero was the high-priest Ananus; and the encomium upon him [52] remotely recalls, though it is not a copy of, that of Thucydides [53] on Pericles. "A man on every ground revered and of the highest integrity, Ananus, with all the distinction of his birth, his rank and the honours to which he had attained, yet delighted to treat the very humblest as his equals. Unique in his love of liberty and an enthusiast for democracy, he on all occasions put the public welfare above his private interests. To maintain peace was his supreme object" and so on. Thus while Athens has coloured the picture of the virtuous hero, Rome has provided a model of vice.

I have attempted to show how the relation of portions of the historian's work to Greek literature—lavish imitation of Thucydides on the one hand, stray echoes of the poets on the other—enables us to detect and isolate the respective contributions of two of his assistants. Elsewhere it is not easy to distinguish how much of the wide acquaintance shown with that literature is due to the author's own reading, how much to the prompting of his subordinates. But between them, besides consulting the necessary pagan sources, they have ransacked, as models of style, historians such as Herodotus, Xenophon, Polybius and Dionysius of Halicarnassus, and, for the speeches interspersed throughout the narrative, Demosthenes and the orators. They have diligently followed the maxim of Horace, " Vos exemplaria Graeca Nocturna versate manu, versate diurna "; [54] and

---

[52] *B.J.* iv. 319 ff.   [53] Thuc. ii. 65.
[54] *Ars Poetica* 268–9.

an English translator of Josephus is grateful for the relief afforded to the tedium of his task by being sent back so often to the great masters.

But there is another side to the picture. With all this indebtedness to the wisdom of the Greeks, all this borrowed plumage and saturation in Greek phraseology, Greek modes of thought and Greek lore, the author has a profound contempt for the race, especially for the contemporary Greek historian. "As for the native Greeks," he writes in the proem to the *Jewish War*,[55] "where personal profit or a lawsuit is concerned, their mouths are at once agape and their tongues loosed; but in the matter of history, where veracity and laborious collection of the facts are essential, they are mute, leaving to inferior and ill-informed writers the task of describing the exploits of their rulers. Let us at least hold historical truth in honour, since by Greeks it is disregarded." Here undoubtedly speaks the historian himself, and not his obsequious Greek assistant. Pro-Roman, in war days at least, our author was; phil-Hellene, never. One seeming exception to this is interesting. The allusion in Agrippa's great speech[56] to "Greeks who, though *noblest of all races under the sun* ... are yet subservient to six rods of a Roman magistrate" comes from the pen not of the author but of the assistant whom I call "α";[57] and here there are significant diversities of reading, suggesting a conflict of opinion between the two. I follow Niese's MS "preeminent in nobility" (προύχοντες εὐγενείᾳ); but the majority of the MSS have "reputed to be preeminent" (προύχειν ... δοκοῦντες), while one of them reads "who are reputed *and are* preeminent," (προύχειν ... δοκοῦντες καὶ ὄντες), as if the assistant had protested and reasserted his proud opinion of his race. In other cases, where the rival claims of style and accuracy are contrasted, we seem to hear two voices speaking in the grudging admission, "Yes, you Greeks are excellent stylists, but

---

[55] *B.J.* i. 16.   [56] *ib.* ii. 365.

[57] *Cf. Ant.* xv. 412 ἔργον ἀξιαφηγότατον τῶν ὑφ' ἡλίῳ (with iv. 114, viii. 49); also the phrase τὸν ἥλιον ὁρᾶν (βλέπειν) xvi. 99, 108, 204.

style is not everything." Thus in the *contra Apionem*,[58] "While, then, for eloquence and literary ability we must yield the palm to the Greek historians, we have no reason to do so for veracity in the history of antiquity."

I ended my lecture yesterday with an encomium on our author's *apologia* for Judaism, the little treatise known as *contra Apionem*. I will conclude to-day by reverting to that same excellent and many-sided work, in another of its aspects. For here, as nowhere else in our author's works, we find the learning of Judaism and of Hellenism side by side, blended and contrasted in a volume of small compass. The writer's patriotic zeal for Judaism dominates the writing, but that zeal leads him to contrast his own religion with the beliefs of other nations and so carries him into some strange by-paths of Greek literature. The work is at once a defence of Judaism, a repository of recondite Greek lore, and an attack on the morality and pretensions of the Greeks, combining just criticism of their faults with an appreciation of the merits of their great philosophers. It matters not how much of this learning the author owes to others: it is sufficient that he has produced an admirable book. His principal opponent, Apion, was an erudite grammarian, and he needed to be well-armed.

I spoke of the work as a repository of Greek lore, and the abstruse knowledge displayed is indeed astonishing. We seem to be moving in the literary circles of Apion's own Alexandria, in which antiquarian problems and questions of doubtful authorship are discussed and the merits of the great masters criticised. Did the Homeric Greeks know the alphabet? "It is a highly controversial and disputed question," we are here told,[59] "whether even those who took part in the Trojan campaign ... made use of letters, and the true and prevalent view is rather that they were ignorant of the present-day mode of writing." Here we have an allusion to the interpretation still debated to-day, of a phrase in the Iliad,[60] σήματα

[58] *Ap.* i. 27, *cf. Ant.* xiv. 2 f.   [59] *Ap.* i. 11.   [60] vi. 168.

λυγρά, "baneful tokens," applied to a message which was to bring about the death of Bellerophon. Did Homer himself commit his poems to writing? No, answers our author, "even he, they say, did not leave his poems in writing. At first transmitted by memory, the scattered songs were not united until later, to which circumstance the numerous inconsistencies of the work are attributable." [61] This is a *locus classicus*, on which Wolf largely relied in his famous *Prolegomena*, produced in 1795, on the origin of the Homeric poems. Similarly the writer knows that the word νόμος does not occur in Homer. "Why, the very word ' law ' was unknown in ancient Greece. Witness Homer, who nowhere employs it in his poems." [62] He knows that a certain lampoon, known as *Tripoliticus* or the " Three states book," attacking Athens, Sparta and Thebes, and put out in the name of Theopompus by an enemy who so successfully imitated his style as to bring him into universal odium, was not really written by Theopompus. [63] He knows of current criticism on the visionary ideals of the *Republic* of Plato, who for all his dignity of character and eloquence " is continually being almost scoffed at and held up to ridicule by those who claim to be expert statesmen." [64]   And, through a brilliant emendation of a corrupt reading of the MSS (νῦν), we learn that he knew the name of an obscure priestess, called Ninus, who was put to death by the Athenians for initiating people into the mysteries of foreign gods. [65]

Beside these recondite allusions, we have at the beginning and close of the work a reasoned criticism of the pretensions and religion of the Greeks. They are untrustworthy as antiquarians, being, in comparison with Egyptians and eastern nations, but a people of yesterday. [66] Their land " has experienced countless catastrophes, which have obliterated the memory of the past; and as one civilization succeeded another the men of each epoch believed that the world began with them. They were late in learning the alphabet and found the lesson difficult " [67] and so on. The dis-

[61] *Ap.* i. 12.   [62] *Ap.* ii. 154 f.   [63] *Ap.* i. 221.   [64] *Ap.* ii. 223.

[65] *ib.* ii. 267.   [66] *Ap.* i. 7.   [67] *ib.* 10.

crepancies between their historians are attributed partly to their
neglect to keep public records, partly to their regard for style rather
than accuracy.[68]   Their records are "mere stories improvised
according to the fancy of their authors." [69]   And then at the close,[70]
introduced with apologies for the comparison of the rival religions
to which opponents have driven him, we have a scathing denunciation
of the gross and immoral Hellenic ideas about their gods, showing
acquaintance with the whole range of Greek mythology.   The cause
of these erroneous conceptions is traced to the neglect of religion by
their legislators and to the licence given to poets and artists; while
it is claimed, as had been claimed by Philo and others before him,
that Plato and the great philosophers derived their higher ideas from
Judaism and were in reality Moses' disciples.[71]

The argument is well reasoned and sustained; the attack is as able
as the defence; and the sentiments, if not all the language, are
undoubtedly the author's own.   If I began by putting in a plea on
behalf of his assistants, I must end by admitting that Josephus
here makes good his claim to have immersed himself in Greek
literature, and has given us a vivid picture of the merits and defects
of Hellenism.

[68] *ib.* 15 ff.   [69] *ib.* 45.   [70] *Ap.* ii. 237 ff.   [71] *Ap.* ii. 168, 257.

JOSEPHUS AND CHRISTIANITY

I approach the subject of my last lecture with hesitation and misgiving. The matter is, on more than one ground, controversial, and the critical problems which it raises are of more than ordinary difficulty. I am reluctant to enter this arena, more especially as I am conscious of having fluctuated in my opinion in the past and, on some points, am still in doubt. But though I have little that is new to contribute to the discussion, the subject could not be wholly avoided.

We have what may be called the older and the newer evidence. The so-called *testimonium Flavianum*—the well-known statement on the Founder of Christianity in the eighteenth book of the *Antiquities*—with two other cognate passages in that work, has been long with us, and though scholars are still far from unanimous concerning its authenticity, the question has been debated for centuries past from almost every conceivable point of view and new arguments are hardly likely to be forthcoming.

It is otherwise with the new evidence which has been brought to light within the last quarter of a century, namely the existence of some strange statements concerning John the Baptist, Jesus and the early Christians in the Slavonic version of the *Jewish War*. These allusions to Christianity were in 1906 translated and discussed by the late Dr. Berendts in Harnack's *Texte und Untersuchungen*,[1] and a German translation which he had completed before his death of the Slavonic version of the first four books of the *War* has now been edited by Professor Grass;[2] the last three books still

[1] *Neue Folge* 14.

[2] Berendts-Grass, *Flavius Josephus vom Jüdischen Kriege, Buch i–iv, nach der slavischen Übersetzung*, Dorpat, Teil I 1924–26, Teil II 1927.

await a translator. Difficult as are the problems connected with the *testimonium* in the *Antiquities*, in this Slavonic version of the *War* we are on even more debatable ground. The theory tentatively put forward by Berendts in his first publication that the Slavonic may have preserved to us the genuine first draft of the *Jewish War*, written by Josephus for eastern readers, was ridiculed by Schürer [3] and few scholars have since seriously considered it. It has, however, found one whole-hearted supporter in Dr. Robert Eisler, whose views have now [1929] been put forth in a work on which he has long been engaged.[3a] Shortly before I had the honour of being invited to deliver these lectures, I was privileged to see a good deal of Dr. Eisler's work in its earlier stages. I therefore find myself in a rather difficult position. I am reluctant to make use of unpublished [3b] materials, even with the author's consent; moreover, I have recently come so closely under the influence of the writer, that I have not been able to form a wholly unbiassed opinion. I must, however, confess that, much as I have learnt from that brilliant scholar, I am far from being converted to all his revolutionary views. In the circumstances, I propose to confine myself mainly to the old and well-worn passages in the *Antiquities* and to touch but lightly on this new and untried ground. The two can be considered independently, and I will not attempt to explain *obscurum per obscurius*.

I will begin with some preliminary observations on three points: the opportunities of Josephus for obtaining correct information, the external conditions under which he wrote as affording reason for reticence, and the liability of his work to Christian interpolation.

(1) Of the main facts of the life and death of Jesus, Josephus cannot have been ignorant. Of him it might almost have been said, as was said of his friend Agrippa by the Apostle Paul when on his trial before Festus and the King: "I am persuaded that none

---

[3] *Theologische Literaturzeitung*, 1906, col. 262–266.

[3a] Ιησους βασιλευς ου βασιλευσας, Lieferung 1–18, C. Winter, Heidelberg 1928–1929.   [3b] i.e. in 1928, when these lectures were delivered.

of these things is hidden from him, for this thing hath not been done in a corner." [4] Yet such information as he may have gained in his earlier Palestinian period, being derived wholly from hearsay report, is likely to have been garbled and imperfect. He would not hear much truth about the Christians on that early visit to Rome in 64, the year of the fire which was falsely laid to their charge. And in Palestine the followers of Jesus possessed as yet no written records, beyond perhaps a collection of sayings of their Master and another collection of Old Testament prophecies with corresponding fulfilments in the events of his earthly life. On the other hand, allowance must naturally be made for the acquisition of fuller information during that period of nearly twenty years that elapsed in Rome between the dates of writing of his two major works. Documents were now available, which, though the Jewish historian may never have looked at them, would be known to any Christian informants with whom he may have come into contact. When the *Antiquities* appeared in the year 93, the Gospel of Mark, written, according to credible tradition, for Roman Christians, was in circulation, and another evangelist, Luke, had recently produced in Rome a narrative both of the life of his Master and of the early Church. It is interesting to recall that three historians were now simultaneously at work in the capital of the Empire: Josephus, writer of the *Jewish Antiquities,* Tacitus the coming historian of the Roman Empire, and Luke the annalist, on a smaller scale, of the infant Church; and that the two latter have been thought to show dependence on the Jewish historian. Tacitus, the earliest external writer, excepting Pliny and Josephus, to allude to Christ and the Christians,[5] is by some authorities believed to have drawn his information from the famous *testimonium*; and Luke, on insufficient

---

[4] Acts xxvi. 26.

[5] *Ann.* xv. 44 " Nero subdidit reos ... quos per flagitia invisos vulgus Christianos appellabat. Auctor nominis ejus Christus Tiberio imperitante per procuratorem Pontium Pilatum supplicio adfectus est; repressaque in praesens exitiabilis superstitio rursum erumpebat, " &c.

grounds in my opinion, is considered to have cursorily perused the last books of the *Antiquities*. A recent writer has suggested that the supposed connexion between the *Acts* and the *Antiquities* may be explained by the evangelist's having heard, rather than read, the later work. Josephus, writes Canon Streeter,[6] "would certainly have recited parts of the *Antiquities* at intervals during the ten years before its publication. Fashionable Rome felt bound in etiquette to attend the recitations of its noble friends; but a parvenu like Josephus would have been only too glad to fill up the back seats with unimportant people like Luke." I do not suggest that he either did so or, if he did, that he would have returned the compliment by sitting at the feet of Luke; but at least there is nothing improbable in his having met him or read, or met others who had read, his work.

From these chronological considerations two inferences may, I think, be drawn. Any allusion to Christianity that may once have stood in the earlier work, the *Jewish War*, is not to be condemned offhand because it is crude and erroneous. On the other hand, any such allusion in the later work, the *Antiquities*, cannot be pronounced an interpolation on the sole ground that it approximates to a Christian creed.

(2) Information being then so readily accessible, mere curiosity would lead Josephus to make inquiries concerning this sect which was already gaining adherents in the upper circles at court. Even as far back as his youthful visit to Rome, they had obtained a footing there, though in a menial capacity: "they of Caesar's household" had then sent their salutations by St. Paul to a distant Church.[7] And now the new religion was shortly to penetrate to the highest quarters and win converts to their peril among the near kinsmen of the Emperor, distinguished persons bearing the same "Flavian" name as the historian himself. To know the facts was one thing, to allude to them in writing was another; was the risk so great as to make complete silence imperative? Christians and Jews,

---

[6] *The Four Gospels* 558.   [7] Phil. iv. 22.

not very carefully distinguished, were alike in disfavour under Domitian, but, except possibly at the opening and certainly in the last year of his reign there is no evidence for actual persecution. In that last year, 95–96, Domitian, in a fit of savagery put to death, among others, his first cousin Flavius Clemens, consul in the previous year, and banished the ex-consul's wife Flavia Domitilla, the emperor's niece, on the charge of "atheism," in other words, as Eusebius says, "for witness to Christ." [8] These proceedings might well have deterred a bolder man than Josephus from uttering anything which might be construed as sympathetic to the new movement. But, in fact, it is important to note that the first edition of the *Antiquities* had been issued two years earlier, in the thirteenth year of Domitian, 93–94. [9] The peril to which such a statement as the *testimonium* might expose its author, had not yet become acute, and the death of Domitian following shortly after that outburst and the altered conditions under Nerva would render subsequent excision unnecessary. The one previous action recorded of Domitian in relation to Christianity might have seemed to the historian to render innocuous a brief and colourless reference to facts which he could hardly ignore. In pursuance of action previously taken by Vespasian, [10] Domitian, as we are told by Hegesippus, [11] had given orders for the destruction of any claimants to descent from David, whereupon certain grandsons of Judas, the brother of the Lord, were brought up to him; but finding them common labourers who did not look for an earthly kingdom, he dismissed them, and, as Eusebius adds, put a stop by edict to the persecution of the Church. In these circumstances Josephus might well expect to make with impunity a passing and not unsympathetic allusion to the murder of James, the brother of "the so-called Christ."

(3) One further preliminary point remains, namely the liability of the work to Christian interpolation and the nature of any such

---

[8] Euseb., *Hist. eccl.* iii. 18; Merivale, *Roman Empire* vii. 152, Lightfoot, *Philippians* (ed. 1) p. 22 and *Apostolic Fathers* Part 1, vol. i.

[9] *Ant.* xx. 267. [10] Euseb., *H.E.* iii. 12. [11] *ib.* iii. 19 f.

interpolation as we may reasonably expect to find. The Jewish historian's works owe their preservation, not to his countrymen, but in the first instance to his Roman patrons, who honoured them with a place in the public library,[12] and subsequently to Christians. Christian scribes have left their obvious marks in occasional marginal glosses in our extant MSS; nor can it be denied that they would be tempted, and, we may probably add, would not scruple, to alter the text of passages hostile to Christianity or even to interpolate passages of a contrary nature, especially after Christianity had become the religion of the state. But here two observations may be made. First, it is illogical to argue, as some critics appear to do, that the Christians preserved the historian's works largely on account of the so-called *testimonium de Christo*, and at the same time that they themselves have interpolated it. They may have tampered with the text, but if the historian's writings owe their preservation to some allusion to Christ, they must have found there already something which met with at least their partial approval. Secondly, any Christian interpolation is likely to betray itself by its style and contents. There is no mistaking the Christian origin of the marginal glosses. We must not expect to find any subtle and artistic forgery by a writer who has masqueraded under the mantle of the historian, and by careful study of his author has endeavoured to palm off his composition upon him. It is true that such skill was not unknown in antiquity, but the successful forger was an extreme rarity. The "Thucydideans" mentioned in my last lecture are not strictly parallel: they aped but did not aim at being mistaken for their model. The one outstanding instance is a work to which Josephus himself alludes,[13] the *Tripoliticus* or "Three states book," a pamphlet attacking Athens, Sparta and Thebes, put out in the name of Theopompus by his enemy Anaximenes, who so successfully imitated that author's style as to bring him into universal odium. But the ordinary Christian scribe lacked such ingenuity; and any characteristic Josephan phrase, any

[12] Euseb. *Hist. eccl.* iii. 9.   [13] *c. Ap.* i. 221.

word used in an un-Christian sense, any statement running counter
to orthodox Christian belief, has *a priori* claim to be considered
authentic.

Now, however disputable may be the authenticity of the well-
known passage on the founder of Christianity in the 18th book of
the *Antiquities,* there is no doubt that Josephus mentions, frankly
and not unfavourably, two persons intimately connected with
Him—John the Baptist and James "the brother of Jesus who was
called Christ" (or in N.T. language "the Lord's brother"). It is
true that he does not himself connect the Baptist with the Christian
movement, but the two movements had so much in common that
his attitude to the one may perhaps not unfairly be taken into
consideration as indicative, to a certain extent, of his attitude
towards the other. The association between the forerunner and
Jesus is too firmly established in the Christian records to be disregarded; Josephus at any rate gives no countenance to modern
theories of an irreconcilable rivalry between them. The authenticity
of these two passages on the Baptist and James is, in my opinion,
beyond question, and they are of considerable interest.

In the first of them [14] Josephus describes the imprisonment and
murder of "John surnamed the Baptist" by Herod Antipas the
Tetrarch. The story is told, apparently without regard to chronological order, in connexion with events in the year 36 A.D., shortly
before the death of Tiberius and about the time of or soon after
the recall of Pilate. Antipas falls in love with Herodias, his
brother Herod's wife, and schemes to contract a secret marriage
with her and to divorce his former wife, the daughter of Aretas.
The aggrieved lady discovers the plot and flees to her father. This
insult to his daughter, together with a frontier dispute, leads to
a battle in which the Tetrarch's army is cut to pieces.

Josephus then proceeds: "Some of the Jews, however, regarded
the destruction of Herod's army as the work of God, who thus

[14] *Ant.* xviii. 5. 2 (116–119).

9*

exacted very righteous retribution for John surnamed the Baptist. For Herod had slain John—a good man who bade the Jews to cultivate virtue by justice towards each other and piety towards God, and (so) to come to baptism; for immersion, he said, would only appear acceptable to God if practised, not as an expiation for specific offences, but for the purification of the body, when the soul had already been thoroughly cleansed by righteousness. Now when men [15] flocked to him—for they were highly elated [16] at listening to his words—Herod feared that the powerful influence which he exercised over men's minds might lead to some form of revolt, for they seemed ready to do anything on his advice. To forestall and kill him seemed far better than a belated repentance when plunged in the turmoil of an insurrection. And so, through Herod's suspicions, John was sent as a prisoner to the fortress of Machaerus and there put to death. The Jews therefore thought that the destruction of Herod's army was the penalty deliberately inflicted upon him by God to avenge John."

The phraseology of this passage betrays the unmistakable marks of the hack employed for this portion of the *Antiquities*. His love of periphrasis is illustrated by the phrase "come to" or "consort with" baptism,[17] for "be baptized," his avoidance of the commonplace vocabulary by the strange words which he uses for "punish," "kill," and "sin";[18] and there are other words found only in this portion of the work.[19] The hand is the hand of the secretary; the voice that prompts it is that of Josephus.

The author does not expressly state that he concurred in the opinion of the Jewish multitudes, but his commendation of John

[15] The MSS have τῶν ἄλλων: Niese reads τῶν ἀνθρώπων.

[16] Eusebius reads " delighted " (ἥσθησαν): the MSS have ἥρθησαν.

[17] βαπτισμῷ συνιέναι.

[18] τινυμένου, else only xvii. 60 (similarly of divine vengeance); κτίννυται, + xv. 118, xvii. 182, xviii. 99; ἁμαρτάς (Ionic for ἁμαρτία), + *Ant.* xviii. 350, and in *Ant.* iii. 204, &c. (the same phrase ἐπὶ παραιτήσει ἁμαρτάδων iii. 238, cf. 221) doubtless from the same hand.

[19] ἀκρόασις, φέρειν ἐπί τινι, " lead to something," *Ant.* xvii. 354, xviii. 128, 169, xix. 61, 242; τοσόσδε is characteristic of this assistant.

as " a good man " and his description of his preaching indicate a sympathy with the victim. I see no reason to question the word ἀγαθόν; my friend Dr. Eisler, in view of the different picture of the Baptist contained in the Slavonic version of the *War*, where he is always spoken of as " the wild man," would regard the word as a Christian correction of an original ἄγριον.

The account here given is not inconsistent with the Gospel narrative, which it supplements rather than contradicts. The tetrarch's adultery with his brother's wife is here mentioned in connexion with, though not as the direct cause of, the Baptist's execution.

In the second passage [20] we have an account of the death of James " the brother of Jesus who was called Christ." Ananus, the newly appointed high-priest, son of the high-priest Ananus or Annas, who in the Gospel narrative is associated with Caiaphas in the trial and condemnation of Jesus, seizes the opportunity of an interregnum in the office of procurator (in 62 A.D.) to put to death, after a perfunctory trial by the Sanhedrin, the half-brother of his father's victim and a formidable rival of his own, who had for over twenty years held a prominent position as head of the primitive Jewish Church in Jerusalem.

The passage runs: " On hearing of the death of Festus, Caesar sent Albinus to Judaea as governor. The King (Agrippa II) at the same time deprived Joseph of the high priesthood and appointed the son of Ananus, also named Ananus, as his successor." Then, after remarking on the unparalleled experience of the elder Ananus in having five sons who all became high-priests, he continues: " The younger Ananus who now, as we said, took over the office, was a rash and extraordinarily daring man, a follower of the sect of the Sadducees, who, as we have already stated,[21] are more ruthless than all Jews in judicial cases. Ananus, then, such being his nature,

---

[20] *Ant.* xx. 197–203.

[21] No previous statement precisely to this effect; but *cf. Ant.* xiii. 294 " The Pharisees (as opposed to Sadducees) are by nature lenient in punishments."

thinking that he had a favourable opportunity—Festus being dead
and Albinus still on the road—summoned the court of the Sanhedrin, brought before it the brother of Jesus who was called
Christ (James was his name) and certain others, and, after
accusing them of transgressing the law, delivered them up to be
stoned. But those who were reputed to be the most moderate of
the citizens and strict observers of the laws took offence at this
action and sent a secret message to the King, petitioning him to
restrain Ananus from similar proceedings in future, as this first act
of his had not been right. Some of them, moreover, went to meet
Albinus on his road from Alexandria and pointed out that it was
illegal for Ananus to convene a meeting of the Sanhedrin [22] without
his consent." The upshot was that Ananus received a reprimand
from Albinus and was deposed from his office by Agrippa.

Nothing in the style of this passage suggests interpolation. The
marked mannerisms of the amanuensis are absent, because in this
twentieth book his services have ceased; but language and tone—
especially the Pharisee's caustic reference to the harshness of the
Sadducees [23]—are thoroughly Josephan.[24] The statement has been
accepted as genuine by most leading scholars, and even by so scep-
tical a critic as Dr. Eisler; but others, including Schürer, have
questioned its authenticity. The only reason, so far as I know,
urged by these critics is the evidence of Origen, which suggests that
there may have been other MSS of Josephus current in his time,
in which this story had been tampered with by Christian hands.
In more than one passage [25] Origen refers to a statement of
Josephus that the murder of James was the cause of the destruction
of Jerusalem, expressing his astonishment that one who witnessed
to so much righteousness in James refused to accept Jesus as the

---

[22] Or rather to pronounce sentence of death, Schürer, *G.J.V.* (ed. 3) ii. 209.

[23] *Cf. B.J.* ii. 166 for their roughness of manner.

[24] One phrase, βαρέως φέρειν (201), is characteristic of this portion of the work,
Ant. xx. 60, 94, *Vita* 50, 189; else only *Ant.* xviii. 241.

[25] *c. Celsum* i. 47, ii. 13, *Comm. in Matt.* x. 17 (on Matt. xiii. 55).

Christ. Now we have a fuller, and less probable, Christian account of the martyrdom of James the Just given us by the second century writer Hegesippus; [26] the victim is there represented as being hurled from the roof of the temple before being stoned and beaten to death, and the story ends with the words " And immediately Vespasian besieged them." Origen, it seems, has blundered and attributed to Josephus what was really written by Hegesippus. It was a natural confusion of two similar names, and was not confined to him; in fact a 4th century Latin version of Josephus has come down to us under this same name Egesippus. The true Josephus, in the traditional text, dates the murder of James four years before the outbreak of war and traces no connexion between the two events. Nor does he, as Origen asserts, pronounce any encomium on the righteousness of James; he is mentioned as one victim among others and that is all. Had the passage been a Christian interpolation, the notice would have been more laudatory.[27]

The passage, indeed, presents other problems; but these do not, I think, affect its authenticity, nor, to my knowledge, are they emphasized by its critics. Of these the most striking is the portrait here given of Ananus. Few would recognise in this " rash and extraordinarily daring man," who took advantage of the absence of a Roman governor to get rid of a religious opponent, the Ananus who is the martyr hero of the Jewish War, whose supreme object was to maintain peace with Rome, and who is eulogised in language worthy of another Pericles.[28] But this is not the only instance of inconsistency in the attitude of the author to individuals in the earlier and in the later work: his relations with Agrippa and the Herodian family had also cooled in the interval. Moreover, Josephus had himself once suffered under this " daring " Ananus, who had been induced to vote for his removal from his command in Galilee;[29] he was now writing his account of those early days

---

[26] *ap.* Euseb., *H.E.* ii. 23.   [27] Lightfoot, *Galatians* (ed. 10) 366 note.
[28] *B.J.* iv. 319 ff.   [29] *Vita* 193 ff.

as an appendix to the *Antiquities* and old memories may have rankled.   Again, who were these Pharisees (for such are clearly intended by the citizens reputed for their moderation and strict observance of the laws) who took offence at the action of Ananus? James would have many friends among those " Pharisees who believed " of whom we read in the Acts of the Apostles,[30] although they had failed some years earlier to persuade him to impose circumcision and the keeping of the whole law of Moses upon Gentile converts.   These would certainly join in the protest, but are not directly in view here; the opposition is said to be prompted by indignation at the high-handed and illegal proceedings of Ananus, not by sympathy for any particular victim.

But at least it is clear that the writer's sympathies are with the " moderates " and that he shows no antagonism to the brother of him " who was called Christ "; just as we may infer from the other passage an attraction towards the Jews who flocked to hear the Baptist, and a bias against Herod who was thought to have met with " a very just retribution."

These two passages lead us to suppose that we may find elsewhere some further mention of the founder of the movement, of " Him who was called Christ."   That phrase by itself suggests some further statement, which an ordinary reader would have a right to expect.

And so I turn to the famous controversial passage in the eighteenth book of the *Antiquities*.[31]   It is brief enough to repeat, familiar as it will be to you:—

" Now about this time arises [32] Jesus, a wise man, if indeed he should be called a man.   For he was a doer of marvellous deeds, a teacher of men who receive the truth with pleasure; and he won over to himself many Jews and many also of the Greek (nation). He was the Christ.   And when, on the indictment of the principal men among us, Pilate had sentenced him to the cross, those who had loved (or perhaps rather ' been content with ') him at the

---

[30] *Acts* xv. 5.   [31] *Ant.* xviii. 63 f.   [32] Or " is born " (γίνεται).

first did not cease; for he appeared to them on the third day alive again, the divine prophets having (fore)told these and ten thousand other wonderful things concerning him. And even now the tribe [33] of Christians, named after him, is not extinct."

Seldom can ten lines have caused such controversy as these. The problem which they present is one of extraordinary difficulty, the arguments on either side being very evenly balanced. For twelve hundred years, from the time of Eusebius down to the sixteenth century, the words were unquestionably accepted and treasured by Christians as the testimony of an outsider, albeit perhaps grudgingly given, to the main articles of their creed. Then ensued the age of criticism, and in the last century the learned world in general had come to reject the whole passage as a Christian interpolation. Recently, as so often happens, there has been a swing of the pendulum; authorities of the first rank, such as Professor Burkitt [33a] in England and Harnack [33b] in Germany, have pronounced it to be authentic, and there has been a tendency to rehabilitate it in whole or in part. Not that there are not still redoubtable antagonists on the other side, notably Schürer, Norden [33c] and, most recently in this country, Professor Zeitlin.[34] Who shall decide where doctors such as these disagree?

I hesitate to express a further opinion, but I have now been led to abandon my former belief that the *whole* is a Christian interpolation. Strong as are the arguments for that theory, those on the other side seem to me to outweigh them. The evidence of language, which, on the one hand, bears marks of the author's style, and on the other is not such as a Christian would have used, appears to me decisive. If the whole is not authentic, there is at least a

[33] Or " race " (φῦλον).

[33a] In *Theologisch Tijdschrift*, Leiden, 1913, pp. 135 ff. So too his colleague Prof. W. Emery Barnes, *The testimony of Josephus to Jesus Christ*, London S.P.C.K. 1920.

[33b] *Internat. Monatsschrift f. Wissenschaft und Technik*, 1913, pp. 1037 ff.

[33c] *Neue Jahrbücher f. d. klass. Altertum*, vol. xxxi, 1913, pp. 637 ff.

[34] *Jewish Quarterly Review*, new series, vol. xviii, No. 3, Jan. 1928, p. 231 ff. " The Christ passage in Josephus."

Josephan nucleus. Either we have the author's complete statement—
studiously concise, equivocal, patronizing and even satirical; or,
as I have, under Dr. Eisler's influence, come to believe, the censor's
hand has been at work, and we are left with the relics of what
was once a fuller and more antagonistic paragraph. In the latter
case, we cannot hope to recover the exact original text; in the
former we cannot say more than that the author may have been
half-heartedly attracted by the personality of One whose followers
had shown such indomitable pertinacity. Were the language such
as to suggest any closer leanings to Christianity, that glowing
eulogy on Judaism in his latest work would forbid such a
belief.

I turn then to the details and must endeavour briefly to summarise
the arguments pro and con, familiar to most of us through centuries
of debate. We have first the external evidence, and then the
internal, the latter under the three heads of context, style and
subject-matter. The external evidence and the argument from
context are the two items most damaging to the counsel for the
defence and I place them in the forefront.

The passage not only stands, without substantial variants, in
all our MSS, dating from the eleventh century onwards, but was
already in existence in its present form in the fourth century, being
quoted more than once by Eusebius.[35] And there the difficulty
begins. Before Eusebius there is no certain trace of it; and such
silence is surprising. The *argumentum e silentio* is always precarious;
yet one might expect that such welcome testimony would be cited
by the early Christian apologists. But there is even more than
this mere negative evidence. Eusebius wrote when Christianity
had recently become the religion of the state, and the censorship
put in force by Constantine against heretical literature raises a
suspicion that his text of Josephus may have been tampered with
or interpolated. If we go back a century earlier, before these

[35] *Hist. eccl.* i. 11, *Dem. evang.* iii. 5, 105.

conditions existed, such suspicions seem to be confirmed. The Alexandrian Origen, writing in the first half of the third century, found indeed allusions in his Josephus to John the Baptist and James, but not only does he not quote the "Christ" passage, but he uses such language as makes it practically impossible to suppose that he knew of it *in its present form*. Only a fragment of Origen's voluminous works have come down to us, and we cannot argue from his silence that he knew of *no* reference in Josephus to Jesus; his lost commentaries would offer other opportunities for such quotation. But how can we reconcile the words in our extant text, "This was the Christ," with the following statements? "The wonder is," writes Origen, "that though he (Josephus) *did not admit our Jesus to be Christ,* he none the less gave his witness to so much righteousness in James," [36] and again "although he *disbelieved in Jesus as Christ* "? [37] This is a formidable argument against the authenticity of the four words in question, and due weight must be given to it. But we are still left with a doubt what Origen found in his text to lead to such a positive assertion, and his allusions to Josephus are peculiar. He is arguing that, whereas Josephus attributed the fall of Jerusalem to the murder of James, he ought rather to have referred it to the crucifixion of Jesus. But, as has been seen, Josephus made no such statement about the death of James; Origen has here either confused Josephus with Hegesippus, or used a text of the Jewish historian which has been interpolated from the Christian writer. His evidence in the one case is thus untrustworthy: how are we to explain the other? The inference that at first suggests itself is that the whole passage about Christ is an interpolation which has crept into the text between the time of Origen and Eusebius, say in the age of Constantine. But that leaves unanswered the question: Whence did Origen learn that Josephus "disbelieved in Jesus as Christ"? The bare phrase "the so-called Christ" in the passage on James seems hardly sufficient

[36] *Comm. in Matt.* x. 17.
[37] *c. Celsum* i. 47.

to account for so dogmatic an assertion. Rather I should infer that he did find some statement in his text concerning Jesus, but not in the form in which the passage has come down to us.

I pass to the internal evidence, and first to the *context,* from which it cannot be isolated. This again *prima facie* suggests an adverse verdict against its authenticity as a whole. The paragraph seems to break the thread of the narrative, the framework of which consists at this point of a series of riots or disturbances (θόρυβοι). It is preceded by two θόρυβοι and followed by two or three more. We have a first disturbance under Pilate, who introduces the standards with the emperor's images into Jerusalem and threatens the Jewish petitioners with death "if they did not desist from turbulence" (*Ant.* xviii. 55—59): a second disturbance when he appropriates the temple treasure for building purposes, his soldiers overpower the turbulent "and so the sedition (στάσις) was quelled" (60–62): the first event occurs in 26 A.D.—the year of Pilate's entry on his office—and the second at some time in the next decade before his recall in 36: then comes the passage about Christ (63 f.): this is followed by a third double disturbance—two scandals in Rome, leading respectively to the crucifixion of the priests of Isis and to the banishment of the Jews (65–84): these events are dated by Tacitus[38] in the year 19 (the departure from chronological order in Josephus is to be noted): lastly, we have a fourth disturbance in Samaria leading to Pilate's recall in 36 A.D. (85–87). In each of these four disturbances the noun θόρυβος or the verb θορυβεῖν occurs, and the opening words of the third, "Now about the same time another calamity disturbed the Jews," seem to connect it directly with the second, leaving no room for our passage, which stands apart and is not linked into the series. The Christian movement itself was doubtless a θόρυβος, the greatest disturbance of all, but in our extant text it is not so presented. This argument carries great weight; it has been powerfully advocated by Norden, who regarded it as conclusive proof that the whole paragraph is

[38] *Ann.* ii. 85.

an interpolation. Yet, serious as it is, this objection is not insuperable. Josephus was a patchwork writer, as appears from this very passage, in which he or possibly an older authority has strung together, not in chronological order, two unconnected sets of riots, one relating to the Jews in Palestine, the other to two religious disturbances in Rome, one of which has nothing to do with the Jews. Whether he or his source is responsible for giving a sort of unity to the whole by the catchword θόρυβος is not clear; but it would be quite in keeping with his methods to break such a framework by the insertion of other matter without bringing it strictly into line with the rest. The Christ passage may have been an after-thought: something had to be said on a thorny subject which had at first been passed over. On the other hand, the Christian movement was so obviously a disturbance of the first magnitude, as it is represented in the New Testament, and as it might so naturally have been represented here, that the explanation is probably to be looked for in another direction, namely in a curtailment by a Christian censor of the original text; the suspicion that such curtailment has taken place is strongly confirmed by a close examination of the language. Here I must repeat that I am indebted to the acuteness of my friend Dr. Eisler who, with great generosity, has permitted me to avail myself of the results of his researches, which will be fully set out in his forthcoming work [now issued, 1929].

Considering the marked peculiarities in the Greek of this portion of the *Antiquities*—the portion, as you may remember, which was entrusted to the hands of the Thucydidean hack—one might expect the style to settle the question of authenticity once for all. The brevity of a passage of under a dozen lines naturally does not give much scope for the mannerisms of the secretary. It does, however, contain one of his characteristic phrases, not found in other parts of Josephus—the phrase " to receive with pleasure." I infer that this amanuensis is still lending his aid. For the rest, practically the whole of the language can be illustrated from Josephus. The criterion of style, to my mind, turns the scale in favour of the authenticity of the passage considered as a whole, if not in every detail. If the text has been multilated and modified, there is at least a Josephan basis.

I must ask your indulgence for dwelling on some *minutiae* of language, but it is only through such details that we can hope to reach the truth in a matter of considerable importance.

Now, what has recently converted me to Dr. Eisler's view is the very opening of our passage—the two little words γίνεται δέ, commonly translated, as I have myself previously translated them, "Now there lived." I always felt I was taking a certain liberty in so translating them, and now it appears that there is no parallel in Josephus (at least both Dr. Eisler and I have failed to find one), perhaps indeed in the whole of Greek literature, for such a meaning. The English rendering "lived" or "flourished" and the rendering of the Old Latin version *fuit* lack all authority. The verb γίνεται, with a personal subject, means either "is born" or, if a predicate is added "becomes" (a cause of something, or the like): with an impersonal subject it means "occurs" or "arises." We have then these two possible renderings, "is born" or "becomes," "proves to be" a source of something or other. The rendering "is born" would be good Greek—I cannot quote an actual parallel from Josephus, though its opposite, τελευτᾷ δέ, occurs [39]—but on chronological grounds seems here highly improbable. Josephus, it is true, is mistaken in his chronology in placing the Roman disturbances after Pilate, but could he have dated the birth of Christ as having taken place about the time of Pilate, who sentenced him to crucifixion, and whose tenure of office was limited to ten years? Nor does the theory of Christian interpolation assist us: the N. T. uses another verb γεννᾶσθαι, not γίνεσθαι, of the birth of Jesus,[40] and a Christian writer is perhaps more likely to have used the past tense, than the historic present, beloved of Josephus. This opening clause γίνεται δέ is in fact thoroughly characteristic of Josephus, but—and here is the important point—it is, invariably I think,

---

[39] *e.g. Ant.* xviii. 39.   [40] Matt. ii. 1 γεννηθέντος.

used to introduce a calamity, disturbance or trouble, or some individual as the source of such trouble. Thus we have "And there arises (γίνεται δέ) a terrible calamity to the Jews in Mesopotamia," [41] "hatred of the Samaritans against the Jews," [42] "a sedition (στάσις) of the Jews of Caesarea against the Syrians," [43] "a popular insurrection"; [44] and again, of the fomenters of such tumults, "And Antiochus again becomes to him a beginning of disturbances (θορύβων)," [45] "And John (of Gischala) becomes a cause of the destruction of this entire party." [46] These parallels [47] create a strong presumption that the phrase was similarly employed here. "And at this time Jesus becomes...," and then a predicate is required, and I think Dr. Eisler is fully justified in inserting some such words as "the beginning of new disturbances," which have been subsequently deleted by a Christian censor, who objected to such a description of his Master.

In the correct interpretation of these two words Dr. Eisler has, I think, found the clue to the interpretation of the whole. For the rest, no large and drastic changes are either desirable or necessary to bring it into line. In view of the Josephan style alterations should be reduced to a minimum; if the author wrote a fuller and more antagonistic statement we cannot hope to recover it. The main point is that Jesus appears to have been represented as a cause of sedition or disturbance, like others who had preceded or followed him, not radically distinguishable in his nature from a Judas or Theudas, except by a certain superiority in his miraculous acts and in his teaching, to which a tribute of admiration of doubtful sincerity is accorded. The several phrases must be briefly reviewed.

To the personal name we should perhaps add the little depreciatory word τις, found in some MSS of Eusebius, and certainly no Christian interpolation—"a certain Jesus."

[41] *Ant.* xviii. 310.   [42] *ib.* xx. 118.   [43] *ib.* xx. 173.
[44] *B.J.* i. 648.   [45] *ib.* i. 99.   [46] *ib.* iv. 208.
[47] I had noted them independently but had failed to grasp their implication.

" A wise man." Josephus might conceivably have been prepared to assign Him a place on the roll of Jewish sages, but again Dr. Eisler's suggestion is plausible, viz. that the censor has been at work and by a slight change produced σοφός out of σοφιστής. That is the word by which the author describes Judas, the founder of a new sect,[48] and others like him, including another Judas and Matthias mentioned in this same portion of the narrative.[49]

" At least if one may call him a man." The phrase has a ring of insincerity, and one must mentally supply, unless Josephus actually himself added, something like " whom his followers call Son of God."

" A doer of marvellous deeds." There is no need for any change here. Dr. Eisler objects that ποιητής elsewhere in Josephus only means a " poet." True, but he has not noticed the fondness of the author's secretary for resolving a simple verb into two, a noun expressing the agent and the auxiliary verb. Just as elsewhere[50] he writes κριτὴς εἶναι " to be a judge (of something) " for the simple κρίνειν " judge," so here he writes ποιητὴς εἶναι for the simple ποιεῖν.

In the next clause, " a teacher of men who receive the truth with pleasure," the hand of this assistant is unmistakable. The phrase " to receive with pleasure," is a hall-mark of this particular scribe, who uses it eight times;[51] outside the three books (xvii–xix) for which he is responsible, it is found nowhere in Josephus, though kindred phrases occur. Josephus has dictated the general tenor of the sentence to his amanuensis who has clothed it in his own words. Christian interpolation is here out of the question: as Harnack has noted, the word ἡδονή, " pleasure," throughout the N. T. and early Christian writings has consistently an evil connotation, and Eusebius has here thought fit to alter " receive with pleasure " into " reverence " (σεβομένων). In Josephus the same associations cling to it, though not quite so universally. In particular, the

---

[48] B.J. ii. 118.   [49] Ant. xvii. 155.   [50] Ant. xix. 217.

[51] Ant. xvii. 329, xviii. 6, 59, 70, 236, 333, xix. 127, 185. A variation on it is ἡδονῇ φέρειν, xvii. 148, &c., also confined to this portion.

phrase "receive with pleasure," in one only out of the eight instances in which it occurs, is used in a good sense.[52] Elsewhere it refers to the welcome given to an impostor (the pseudo-Alexander),[53] to Judas the Galilaean in his rash revolt which led to the nation's ruin,[54] to a plot for the seduction of a Roman matron,[55] to plans of conspiracy,[56] and to the malicious pleasure afforded by the news of the death of two Roman emperors.[57]

Such are the base associations of a phrase here applied to "men who receive the true things with pleasure." If Josephus or his secretary can select no more dignified term than this, no very high commendation can be intended. What is truth in the author's estimation? He does not here employ the abstract term ($\dot{\eta}$ $\dot{\alpha}\lambda\dot{\eta}\theta\epsilon\iota\alpha$), which he uses for instance in his constant assertions of his own veracity, and which in the N. T. has such profound signification. He is not corroborating the whole body of Christian doctrine as formulated in a creed. He is content with the vaguer "true things" ($\tau\dot{\alpha}\lambda\eta\theta\tilde{\eta}$). Harnack suggests that he may be thinking of the sermon of the mount, which at all times deeply impressed Jewish philosophers. But again the question of text arises, and a highly ingenious restoration has been suggested.[58] Emendations are always precarious, but in this case the change required could not be simpler. The obliteration, whether by design or accident, of the middle bar of the capital letter A would convert ΤΑ ΑΗΘΗ "the unusual" into ΤΑΛΗΘΗ "the true." With this reading the author will have spoken of the followers of Jesus as "persons who hail the abnormal with delight." Their Master's actions were paradoxical, his teaching *bizarre*. This suggestion is supported by the fact that the adverbs $\dot{\alpha}\lambda\eta\theta\tilde{\omega}\varsigma$ and $\dot{\alpha}\dot{\eta}\theta\omega\varsigma$ are actually confused elsewhere in Josephus.[59]

[52] *Ant.* xviii. 59 $\dot{\eta}\delta$ον$\tilde{\eta}$ $\delta\dot{\epsilon}\xi\epsilon\sigma\theta\alpha\iota$ τὸν $\theta\dot{\alpha}$νατον (of the Jewish petitioners before Pilate).

[53] *Ant.* xvii. 329.   [54] *ib.* xviii. 6.   [55] *ib.* xviii. 70.   [56] *ib.* xix. 185.

[57] *ib.* xviii. 236, xix. 127.

[58] By Heinichen, as long ago as 1870, and revived by Dr. Eisler.

[59] *B.J.* vi. 403, the Roman victors, finding none to oppose them, were "truly," or, according to other MSS. "unusually" perplexed.

"And he won over to him many Jews and many also of the Greek (community)." No change is needed here. The repetition of "many," the neuter τὸ Ἑλληνικόν,[60] and the use of ἐπάγεσθαι for "win converts" are all thoroughly Josephan; it is significant that the nearest parallel to the last in this portion of the work occurs in connexion with the impostor, the pseudo-Alexander, who won over all the Jews with whom he conversed in Crete to believe in him.[61] The statement about the Greeks would be impossible for a Christian, who would know that his Master's missionary activity was confined to "the lost sheep of the house of Israel."[62] The extension of the preaching to the Gentiles was the work of His disciples and their decision was not reached without keen controversy. The anachronism is, however, a welcome testimony to the wide dissemination of Christianity before the end of the first century.

"He (or "this") was the Christ." Whatever may be the origin and meaning of these words, they cannot, in this writer and in this context, be regarded as a profession of the historian's religious belief. Are they an interpolation? A Christian might rather be expected to write "this *is* the Christ." More probably Josephus wrote them himself or something like them. I was formerly inclined to explain them as a mere identification of the particular person intended—"This was the *Christus* (or *Chrestus*)[63] of whom you have heard tell." No fewer than twenty persons bearing the name of Jesus are mentioned in Josephus; and he constantly interjects such clauses to identify a particular individual: "David... this was the father of Solomon," "Herod, and this was the tetrarch of Galilee"[64] and so on. But the identification usually immediately follows the name and is not separated from it as in the present instance. If this explanation be rejected, we must fall back on

---

[60] *B.J.* ii. 268.   [61] *Ant.* xvii. 327.   [62] Matt. xv. 24.

[63] *Cf.* Suetonius, *Claudius* 25, "Judaeos impulsore Chresto assidue tumultuantes Roma expulit."

[64] Jos., *B.J.* v. 137, *Ant.* xviii. 240, and so frequently.

Jerome's reading, "was believed to be the Christ" (*credebatur* =
ἐνομίζετο), as what Josephus wrote, and regard the word "was"
as a Christian correction. You may remember the conflict of
readings in a passage quoted in a previous lecture,[65] where the
Greeks are, according to different MSS, either "the noblest of
races" or "reputed to be the noblest" or "both reputed and really
the noblest."

The remainder of the paragraph need not long detain us. "On
the indictment of our principal men Pilate sentenced him to the
cross." "The principal men" is common form in Josephus, though
I am not sure that the "our" can be paralleled. The responsibility
for the sentence is laid upon Pilate's shoulders. "Those who were
content with him at the first did not cease." The terseness of the
phrase is ambiguous and suggests possible curtailment by the
censor.[66] If there has been no erasure, "cease" will mean "cease
to exist as a corporate body," like the final words "is not yet
extinct." Though Norden is incorrect in stating that ἀγαπᾶν in
Josephus never means "love," it is true that this particular secretary
only uses it in its classical depreciatory sense of "be content with."[67]
And so we must render it here: his deluded followers "put up
with" such a Master. "For he appeared to them on (lit. "having")[68]
a third day alive again, the divine prophets having (fore)told
these and ten thousand other wonderful things concerning him."
There is no difficulty about this, if, as Dr. Eisler suggests, we may
suppose that the original text was in *oratio obliqua*, as an assertion
not of the historian, but of the Christians. The hyperbole "ten
thousand other things" is thoroughly Josephan and the exaggeration
here has something of a sneer. But, as Dr. Eisler again acutely
suggests, the statement is interesting as an apparent testimony to
the existence of that collection of "Logia" or Old Testament

---

[65] p. 121.

[66] Dr. Eisler would insert " to create a tumult."   [67] *Ant.* xviii. 60, 242.

[68] There is no exact parallel, but Josephus uses ἔχειν (ἔτη) of *age, Ant.* ix. 94, xv. 89;
cf. *Ant.* vii. 1 δύο ἡμέρας ἔχοντος ἐν τῇ Σεκέλλα.

prophecies relating to Christ which is believed to have formed the earliest literature of the primitive Church. "And even now the tribe of Christians, named after him, is not extinct." [69] In the extant text he refrains from adding "unfortunately," but one can almost hear it; the word "tribe" is distinctly disparaging and cannot come from a Christian hand. The Christians regarded themselves as a community or brotherhood with no racial barriers.

That is the solution of the problem, to which, after much wavering in the past, I have, thanks to the expert guidance and acute insight of my friend Dr. Eisler, finally been led. The paragraph in the main comes from Josephus or his secretary, but the Christian censor or copyist has, by slight omissions and alterations, so distorted it as to give it a wholly different complexion. The solution seems to me to satisfy all requirements. It accounts on the one hand for the Josephan style, on the other for the unqualified assertion of Origen and for the omission of the early Christian apologists to quote what they knew to be no testimony to Christ; it meets Norden's objection of lack of formal connexion with the context; and the restored text is in keeping with what a Jew like Josephus may be expected to have written.

It may be asked what evidential value the passage then possesses as a testimony to the truth of the cardinal tenets of Christianity. Here one must admit that the final allusion to the resurrection and the fulfilment of prophecy—whether regarded as an objective and obviously incredulous statement of the historian himself,[70] or, as is more probable, as the report of "those who were content with Him at the first" [71]—is in any case based on information derived from Christian sources. It cannot be claimed as *external* witness to the facts in question: it is a repetition of what the writer had heard from the lips of believers. On the other hand, the Jewish historian does bear his own witness, which a Christian may well

[69] οὐκ ἐπέλιπε, as in *Ant.* xv. 2 (with participle).   [70] With the MS reading ἐφάνη.
[71] With the emendation φανῆναι and consequential changes.

welcome, to the "extraordinary" nature of the acts and the teaching of Jesus, and to the wide diffusion of His followers in his own day. His apparent allusion to that early Christian collection of "Logia," or Old Testament passages which found their fulfilment in Jesus—a work whose existence has been inferred on other grounds—is also highly valuable.

I confess that I find the solution offered more satisfying to mind than heart. In presenting it I feel rather like a traitor to my own camp, to that long line of Christian writers in the past who either regarded Josephus as another Balaam, an unwilling and inspired witness to truths which did not express his own convictions, or actually hailed him as a convert and admitted his works into the canon of Scripture. But I fear we cannot accept either William Whiston's belief that he was an Ebionite Christian, or even Laqueur's fanciful idea that, when his fame as an author was imperilled by the criticisms of his rival Justus, he made overtures to the Christians by inserting this paragraph, and threw, not himself, but his *Antiquities*, into their arms, to ensure their preservation.[72]

I have left myself little time to speak of the new and puzzling Slavonic materials recently brought to light. My remarks on this subject will be deliberately brief and non-committal. I do not feel competent to express a considered opinion, and my main reason in alluding to it at all is to direct your attention to the masterly forthcoming work of my friend Dr. Eisler.

In 1906 the late Dr. Berendts gave us a German rendering of seven passages in the Slavonic version of the *Jewish War* relating to the beginnings of the Christian movement, and raised the question, Can these be the work of Josephus—relics of that primitive Semitic edition written for eastern readers? Critics scoffed, but criticism was premature pending a fuller knowledge of the text as a whole. Now we have Dr. Berendts' version of the first four books of the *War*, edited by Professor Grass. What do we find?

---

[72] *Der jüd. Historiker Fl. Josephus* 274 ff.

Well, we have a version differing from the familiar Greek text in the way both of defect and excess. It is considerably shorter: on the other hand it contains some twenty or more substantial additions. It lacks the Greek proem, and throughout the work a large number of sections are either wholly missing or appear in an abbreviated form. The shorter text is an important, and may prove the decisive factor in the problem; but it is the surplus matter which has hitherto attracted most interest. This is of a miscellaneous character, and some of it is undoubtedly not the work of Josephus. Two passages relate to the historian himself: we have what appears to be a frank statement of the ruse with the lots by which he saved his life at Jotapata,[73] and a fuller speech to his Galilaean troops.[74] With this last we may connect short speeches of the Zealots over the bodies of the murdered high priests.[75] Rather similarly, where the Greek merely mentions a dream of Herod, the Slavonic describes it;[76] elsewhere we are given the dream of another Herod with its interpretation,[77] and we remember that Josephus was a believer in dreams. Where the Greek text mentions that tremendous oaths were taken by the novice on admission to the order of the Essenes, the Slavonic specifies the oaths.[78] Then we have moralizings on Divine providence, with some strange *Haggadah* on the story of Abraham and Lot;[79] further moralizing on Herod's sins and punishment;[80] on the Zealots' disregard of the warnings of Scripture and the lessons of history.[81] Of thoroughly Jewish appearance is the account of a secret debate held by the priests in the time of Herod the Great on the interpretation of Daniel and the expected Messiah.[82] An allusion elsewhere[83] to the "abomination (of desolation) in the holy place" suspiciously resembles N.T. language, though dependent in part on the original prophecy. In Roman history, we have mention of a ruse of Vitellius at the battle of

---

[73] Passage (15) in the Appendix to the Loeb Library translation, vol. iii.
[74] (14) *ibid.*   [75] (17).   [76] (1).   [77] (11).
[78] (10).   [79] (6).   [80] (8).   [81] (18).
[82] (2).   [83] (16).   [84] (19).   [85] (4) and (5).

Bedriacum,[84] and two curious outbursts against the venality of the Latins.[85]

And so we come to the allusions to Christianity. Neither John the Baptist nor Jesus is named: they are referred to respectively as the Wild Man and the Wonder-worker. The Wild Man is represented as the leader of a political movement, summoning the nation to regain their freedom by "the way of the Law"; the opening of his activity is thrown back to the time of Archelaus, some 20 years earlier than in the N.T.; he pronounces doom on Philip and reproves Herod (Antipas) for marrying his deceased brother's wife, Herodias, and his outspoken condemnation leads, as in the N.T., to his death; his extreme asceticism is described, including abstinence from unleavened bread at Passover.[86] The Wonder-worker, who is introduced with the same phrase as in the *Antiquities* "if it is permissible to call him a man," is described as sojourning and performing miraculous cures on the Mount of Olives—nothing is said of a Galilaean ministry. His followers, including 150 closer disciples, vainly urge him to lead a revolt against the Romans. The Jewish leaders report matters to Pilate; the governor, whose dying wife had been healed by the Wonder-worker, arrests and, on a first hearing, releases him, but is subsequently induced by a bribe of 30 talents from the Jews (a curious distortion of the Gospel story) to deliver him to them for crucifixion.[87] Then we hear of the growth of the Christian movement among the lower classes under Claudius and attempts to suppress it.[88] We have an amazing statement about an additional inscription round the outer wall of the Holy Place, to the effect that " Jesus did not reign as King: he was crucified by the Jews for announcing the destruction of the city and the desolation of the Temple." [89] We are told of rival interpretations of that oracle concerning the expected world-ruler who was to come from Judaea: " some interpreted it of Herod, others of the crucified Wonder-worker, others of Vespasian." [90] Lastly, we have a statement, clearly derived

[86] (9) and (11).   [87] (12).   [88] (13).   [89] (20).   [90] (22).

from the Gospel of Matthew, about the rending of the veil of the temple and other portents at the crucifixion.[91]

What are we to make of this strange production? Is it all a hoax—another " Glozel find "? The *prima facie* evidence against it is not to be denied: the lateness of the Slavonic MSS containing it, the derivation of the text from a Greek MS or MSS of a type regarded by Niese as " inferior," the lack of clear attestation in early writers, the patent or apparent dependence, in places, on the New Testament. To the instances already mentioned of such dependence we must probably add the story of Herod Philip and Herodias;[92] while the reasons given by the Roman procurators for not taking action against the early Christians remind us of the counsel of Gamaliel as reported in the Acts of the Apostles,[93] and the words of Josephus to his troops suspiciously resemble St. Paul's advice to the Ephesian Church.[94] Here indeed are grave difficulties to be encountered. What is to be said on the other side? I would single out three points which call for explanation from those who would reject the whole as untrustworthy: the occasional occurrence of Josephan phraseology, the predominant Jewish colouring, and to a certain extent the " omissions " or, perhaps we should say, the shorter text. The absence from the Slavonic of the Greek proem is perfectly natural in the first Aramaic edition; indeed I should have expected a still shorter text. The numerous " omissions " in the body of the text are doubtless in part due to curtailment of the Slavonic translator, who failed to understand his original; but other instances, by their length or by the coherence of the absent topics, suggest that his exemplar was a shorter edition lacking the author's later insertions.

I must not, however, pursue the subject, but would rather call your attention to the work of the leading living authority, who has brought to bear upon it his stores of learning, keen and imaginative insight, and years of study. Dr. Robert Eisler has, *inter alia*,

[91] (21).   [92] (11).   [93] (13) with *Acts* v. 38 f.

[94] (14): *cf.* Eph. iv. 26–32.

reconstructed the romantic story of how the text of Josephus found its way into Russia and was used as a propagandist work at the time of the " Judaizing heresy " in the fifteenth century. Working back from that date, he discovers links with this peculiar text in earlier ages, in the obscure sect of the " Josephinists," in allusions to the " genuine " and " spurious " Josephus, which he connects with an orthodox recension of the text in the time of Constantine, and finds echoes of it in the 4th century Latin translator known as " Egesippus." After carefully sifting the text and eliminating later accretions, he believes that the remainder goes back to the author's first rough Greek draft of his Aramaic edition. The assumption of such an intermediate stage—a rough draft interposed between the lost Aramaic and the polished extant Greek—is necessary to his theory, and is not unnatural. Moreover, he finds traces of the original Aramaic underlying the Greek. Largely on the basis of this text he has ventured to challenge the chronology represented by the Gospel records and to rewrite the story of the first beginnings of the Christian movement. It is a bold venture, and I, for one, am far from agreeing with his reconstruction of the history, but he is a doughty antagonist and his critics will need all their armour to refute him.

GENERAL INDEX

INDEX OF PASSAGES

References to Josephus in the text are to the sections of Niese which appear in subsequent editions. References to the older chapter-divisions are appended in brackets below.